to
R
inscribed
1st ed.

19.99

signed
inscribed

1/7

The Witness Trees

The Witness Trees

Lithuania
by Myra Sklarew

Translated into Yiddish
by David Wolpe

For Dr. Gertrude Ticho

In appreciation and with my best wishes,

Myra Sk____

5761

For Peter Magnes and Lois Magnes

*I'm so pleased to write my message
near Dr. Ticho's and so glad to
have met
you both —
Best,*

M S

A Dora Teitelboim Center
for Yiddish Culture Publication

Cornwall Books
New York • London

Cornwall Books
440 Forsgate Drive
Cranbury, NJ 08512

Cornwall Books
16 Barter Street
London WC1A 2AH, England

Cornwall Books
P.O. Box 338, Port Credit
Mississauga, Ontario
Canada L5G 4L8

The paper used in this publication meets the requirements
of the American National Standard for Permanence of Paper
for Printed Library Materials Z39.48-1984.

Library of Congress Cataloging-in-Publication Data

Sklarew, Myra.
    The witness tree : Lithuania poems / by Myra Sklarew ; translated into
Yiddish by David Wolpe.
        p.   cm.
    "A Dora Teitelboim Center for Yiddish Culture Publication."
    ISBN 0-8453-4525-7 (alk. paper)
    1. Sklarew, Myra—Translations into Yiddish.   2. Holocaust, Jewish
(1939–1945)—Lithuania—Poetry.   3. World War, 1939–1945—
Lithuania—Poetry.   4. Jews—Lithuania—Poetry.   5. Lithuania—
Poetry.   I. Wolpe, David.   II. Title.

PS3569.K57 W58   2000
811'.54—dc21   00-059622

PRINTED IN THE UNITED STATES OF AMERICA

What is The Dora Teitelboim Center for Yiddish Culture?

Dora Teitelboim was an internationally renowned Yiddish poetess, whose fiery social motifs sang and wept joys and sorrows and above all, the love of mankind. Ms. Teitelboim, the poetess for whom "the wind itself speaks Yiddish," had a dream of establishing an organization that would promote Yiddish poetry and prose to a new generation of Americans by making Yiddish works more accessible to the American public, thereby cultivating a new harvest of Yiddish educators, writers, speakers, and performers.

The Center continues the dream of its namesake through publishing high-quality translations of Yiddish literature, running an annual cultural writing contest, promoting the rich texture and beauty of Jewish culture through lectures and cultural events, and producing documentary film and radio programming.

Yiddish has for one thousand years been the language of the troubadour, poet, sweatshop toiler, revolutionary, and dreamer. Yiddish became the vehicle of secular Jewish life to give solid footing to a people without territory of their own. Although Yiddish fell victim to an unnatural death as a result of the Holocaust, it is experiencing a renaissance not seen for many years. This book is part of a series of books published in English and Yiddish about the Holocaust, and stands as a powerful testament to the beauty and endurance of the *mame-loshn* (mother tongue) in the face of the Nazi attempt to wipe it out. The beauty of this volume is that it upholds the poet's duty to remember the past and to remind future generations that this genocide and all other genocides will not be repeated by rejecting silent acquiescence in the face of brute force. Let us be alert that such atrocities be not repeated, whether in the name of nationalism, fighting terrorism, or democracy.

January, 2000

DAVID WEINTRAUB
Executive Director
www.yiddishculture.org

Contents

Acknowledgments

Grateful acknowledgment is made to Richard Schaaf at Azul Editions for permission to reprint the title poem of *Lithuania: New & Selected Poems* and for having the faith in this work from the beginning to publish it as part of this distinguished poetry series. Richard Schaaf has labored in the vineyard of poetry, devoting years of his life to bringing forth the works—in some cases translating them—of Rainer Maria Rilke, Pablo Neruda, Pedro Mir, Cristina Peri Rossi, Jack Hirschman, Marjorie Agosin, and Jacques Roumain. He has been a champion of the poetry of witness.

Thanks to Judith Cohen of the United States Holocaust Memorial Museum's Photo Archives for her excellent, knowledgeable help in locating photographs for this book.

Part 8 of *Lithuania* is based in part on "Kalavrita of the Thousand Antigones" by Charlotte Delbo, from *Days and Memory* (Marlboro, Vermont: The Marlboro Press, 1990).

The concluding nine lines of *Lithuania* are from the Book of Job.

The first three sections of *Lithuania* received the Anna Davidson Rosenberg Award in December 1993 from the Judah Magnes Museum.

To Itche Goldberg whose dedication to Yiddish culture blossoms each day in new sprouts of respect and interest in Yiddish in everyone he touches; and to David Wolpe whose noble survival of the Holocaust and whose mastery of Yiddish literature keeps the Yiddish light shining brightly.

Introduction: On Jewish Lithuania and a Shtetl called Keidan

DOVID KATZ

There are numerous poems in the English language on the Holocaust—the unfathomable mass genocide of European Jewry that marred not only the recently lapsed century, but all of modernity. The widespread illusion that technological advancement and science necessarily make for a better world has forever been debunked.

Predictably, most Holocaust poetry in English is written from a vast geographic, conceptual, and cultural distance. It tends to take the form of the elegy, and to speak in grandiloquent terms of good and evil, and of the human capacity for mass murder. Not infrequently, sentimental praise is heaped on some timeless, placeless "general Judaism" that might just as well be construed as, say, present-day American Jewish life (or perhaps Israeli life, or maybe even ancient Israelite society).

But the civilization that was destroyed in its native homeland was (and in its hopeful remnants still is) a highly unique Jewish society characterized by the rich Yiddish heritage and breathtaking ideological diversity.

Predictably, Yiddish poetry on the *Khurbn* (the Yiddish word for "Holocaust") is written from a much closer perspective. The poets who are themselves survivors write firsthand about the down-to-earth horror. Moreover, they, like Yiddish writers who emigrated before the war, grew up in an environment steeped in the Yiddish civilization of the now-annihilated communities. Their poetry reflects an irreplaceable intimacy with pre-war East European Jewish life.

What you are holding in your hands is something very new and different. It is an English Holocaust poem written by an American-born poet who has sought out genuine Yiddish culture in America, and, most relevant to the point here, one who embarked on the poem

11

Students of the "Yanover yiddisher folkshul" (the Janove Yiddish grammar school) are performing the second act of the play "Wild Flowers" on Chanukah eve, December 8, 1928. Photo credit: YIVO Institute for Jewish Research, courtesy of USHMM Archives.

Lithuania as a direct result of her journeys to her ancestral homeland. If you come here and speak to Jewish survivors and non-Jewish witnesses, you too will learn of the unspeakable horrors that occurred as soon as Soviet forces fled eastward in the wake of the advancing German army during that last week of June 1941. Many local fascists committed atrocities before the Germans even arrived. When they did arrive, the killings became "well organized," although local units were asked (and cheerfully agreed) to do the actual shooting.

In fact, the Nazis' "Final Solution" was first enacted en masse here in Lithuania in 1941, following the German invasion of Soviet-held territories. At the time, mass-murder machinery in the concentration camps had not yet been put into large-scale operation. But the summer of 1941 in Lithuania quickly convinced the Nazis how easy it would be to cunningly enlist elements of the local population to "do the dirty work." Lithuania had been made into a Soviet republic a year before, in 1940. It was now touted that "all Jews are communists" in a country that had endured a bitterly resented Soviet occupation, during which Soviet authorities deported to Siberia many "bourgeois" elements (owners of the larger businesses in many towns). As it turns out, more Jews than Christians, pro rata, were exiled, but facts become insignificant in the face of mass hysteria. Needless to say, close to one hundred percent of the Jewish men, women, and children butchered in the summer and autumn of 1941 had absolutely nothing to do with the Soviet occupation or its excesses. Who could be further from communism than the rabbi whose decapitated head was placed in a shop window, or the one whose headless body was found still seated by an open volume of the Talmud? These references in the poem are historically (if horrifyingly) accurate.

History has yet to explain how even such mass hysteria could lead to the events that transpired: hundreds of thousands of unarmed civilians, including all the women, children, old people and sick people—in other words the entire population of the singled-out race—were (in quick succession) humiliated, imprisoned, tortured, and murdered, and their property stolen. Around a quarter of a million Lithuanian Jews were shot and dumped, often still breathing, in the large mass graves that dot the countryside of modern Lithuania and Belarus (territories that had belonged to pre-1939 Lithuania, Eastern Poland, and Belorussian S.S.R., and that had been incorporated into the U.S.S.R. in 1939 and 1940.) Ninety-five percent of

A street scene in Keidan showing Jewish shops with signs in Yiddish and Lithuanian, circa 1935. Photo credit: Yad Vashem Photo Archives, courtesy of USHMM Photo Archives.

13

Lithuanian Jewry perished, the largest percentage of any country in Europe during the Holocaust.

Lithuanian Jewish civilization was brought to an abrupt and macabre end by an orgy of barbarism in which Jews,—*because* they were Jews—were beaten, cut, and shot to death with a sadism and glee that sometimes baffled even the German SS and the *Einsatzgruppen* who were aiming for a much more "orderly" and less ostentatiously crude method of mass murder. (And it did become more "orderly" as the months of summer and autumn progressed.)

If you come here you will also learn of instances of brave (if hopeless) resistance by Jews, and also learn of magnificent acts of heroism on the part of individual Lithuanians who risked themselves and their families. A fascist with an automatic weapon can murder thousands of unarmed incarcerated civilians in a very short time. But to save one Jew meant risking everything and living in constant fear of death. The rescuers too (alas, there were all too few) are also referred to in *Lithuania*.

Lithuania is a Holocaust poem that describes what actually happened, discovered by inspection of the killing sites and by speaking to survivors and witnesses. That is why the full-blooded, sickening minutiae of the mass murder are revealed here uncensored, and that is ultimately why this is a very special poem.

Lithuania is also unique because it has been translated from English into Yiddish by a leading Yiddish poet, David Wolpe of Johannesburg. Wolpe, whose ninetieth birthday was celebrated by the Yiddish literary world in 1998, is himself a native of Keidan (pronounced kay-DAN), the Lithuanian town most frequently mentioned in *Lithuania*. He migrated to Palestine in 1930, and returned home to Lithuania in 1937, suffering through and witnessing acts of barbarity described herein. His own Yiddish Holocaust work is considered a precious contribution to modern Yiddish poetry, and he is rightly judged to be one of today's Yiddish masters.

This bilingual edition, featuring a translation *into* the Yiddish, is symbolic of the failure of the Nazis and their collaborators to destroy Yiddish culture.

The active Jewish life of the small but vibrant Jewish community in Lithuania today is also a symbol of near-miraculous Jewish survival. Many of the Jews you will meet in the cities of Lithuania and the towns and villages of nearby Belarus have much to say about the richness of pre-war Jewish life. In Belarus especially, you will meet

14

many who are far to the left (proudly communist) or far to the right (deeply religious) of the American Jewish "center." The last elderly remaining Jews here are ever so happy to be visited by foreigners. It is a spontaneous, exuberant happiness. They are the forgotten survivors who never made it to the west or to Israel, and who never benefited seriously from any of the German or Swiss compensation programs. Let them not be forgotten as long as they are here.

※

For all the Holocaust museums and educational programs, there is a grave danger that the truth about the Holocaust will be remembered only by a few specialists and only in an abstract way.

There is, however, the even greater danger that the living civilization that thrived in Eastern Europe will disappear.

Preservation of the culture of the victims is at least as important as learning about their annihilation.

It is therefore appropriate to turn to some aspects of the history and culture of Jewish Lithuania, and to its *shtetl* Keidan, whose Holocaust forms the unifying theme of Myra Sklarew's *Lithuania*.

※

Yiddish culture never had an army or a navy. Still, East European Jewry developed firm geographic notions based on internal Jewish cultural criteria. The borders arrived at rarely match modern political boundaries. Jewish Lithuania (*Lita,* pronounced *Litteh* in Yiddish), corresponds to an area that today includes Lithuania, Latvia, Belarus, parts of northern Poland and even small chunks of the Ukraine and Russia. In fact, the territory of Lita more closely matches up with the lands captured by the Grand Duchy of Lithuania by the mid-fourteenth century, a fact that immediately reveals the antiquity of Jewish settlement of the area.

In the medieval period, central Europe was sinking in (largely German) hatred of Jews, manifested in the Crusades that began in 1096, when the bands seeking to recover the Holy Grail in Jerusalem decided to murder the "local infidels" first. Then came the massacres following the Black Death of 1348 and 1349, when Jews were accused of poisoning the wells. There were many other outbreaks of anti-Jewish violence.

During much of this period, things were much better in the Slavic and Baltic lands of Eastern Europe. Compared to their western counterparts, rulers of Poland and (especially) Lithuania were "modern liberals" who issued edicts of religious and cultural toleration, as well as physical protection, in order to encourage Jewish migration (which they sought largely for economic reasons). The charters granted to the Jews by the Polish prince Boleslav V in 1264, and the Lithuanian grand duke Vytautas (Vitold) in 1388 and 1389, were among the confidence-building measures that paved the way for mass migration of Jews eastward, and ultimately led to a uniquely Eastern European development of Ashkenazic culture.

The single major characteristic of Lithuanian Jewish civilization is love of learning for its own sake. In earlier times, this study-based society had Talmudic scholarship at its core. Many moderns have serious misconceptions about what the Talmud is. Although it has its narrow religious components, Talmudic literature is a vast and variegated literature, written in two languages (Hebrew and Aramaic), and studied in a third (Yiddish). The extensive, continually growing Talmudic literature (mainly in the genre of the commentary upon a given text) covers every sphere of life, from prayer to personal behavior and ethics; from the structure of the ancient Temple in Jerusalem to the days of the yearned for Messiah-to-come. The overwhelmingly greatest part of Talmudic literature, however, fits into what we would today call jurisprudence. It is a literature based on debate of intricate points of law and legalistic logic that calls for sharp thinking, analytic originality, and acute memory. This was a society where the most prestigious "thing" a rich man could buy for himself and his family was not a vehicle or a property, not gold or jewels, but a son-in-law who had true academic talent for Talmudic study.

In the sixteenth century, poor Lithuanian Jewish communities were giving their last pennies to "import" prominent scholars from other countries. By the seventeenth century, their yeshivas (higher Talmudical academies) were themselves turning out genuine masters, such as Shabsay Hakoyheyn (affectionately known as "the Shakh," an acronymic from the name of his best-known commentary) and Moyshe Rivkes.

By the eighteenth century, Vilna, the historic capital of Lithuania, was already affectionately known as "Yerusholayim d'Lita" or Jerusalem of Lithuania. The greatest Talmudic scholar of the last millennium was the renowned Gaon of Vilna, Eyliohu (Elijah) son of Shloyme-Zalmen Kremer. The Vilna Gaon (known in Yiddish as *der vilner goen*) lived from 1720 to 1797.

The Gaon's methodology bears a striking resemblance to many of the methods of modern literary and textual scholarship. Where prevalent rabbinic style often resorted to far-fetched "clever" escapes from contradictory or unclear passages, the Gaon often dared to declare that over hundreds (and in some cases thousands) of years of copying and recopying, many errors crept into the texts. He often suggested emending the text, as modern scholars might put it, or he would frequently reconstruct a hypothesized proto-text using context, logic, comparison of similar surviving passages, and of course, common sense.

But the Gaon's contributions did not stop with Talmud. He wrote tracts on grammar, trigonometry, and other secular sciences. Today a debate rages as to whether or not his methods contributed, directly or indirectly, to the secularization movements that were knocking at the door of Lithuanian Jewry. One thing is certain however: the Gaon's and Lithuanian Jewry's love of learning and knowledge could not confine itself to the traditional yeshiva curriculum. That the greatest Lithuanian Jewish scholar himself "crossed the border" says much in itself.

The Gaon and his close disciples led the war on Hasidism, the new mystical Jewish movement that emanated from Podolia in the Ukraine and spread through large parts of the areas to the south of Lithuania. As these Lithuanian Jewish scholars saw it, Hasidism was fanatical, intellectually lightweight, stressing long, ecstatic prayer sessions to avoid the hard mental toil of scholarship. Perhaps worst of all, the Hasidim were seen to deify a *rebbe* (a dynastically reigning grand rabbi thought to have special links with the divine). The majority of Lithuanian Jews, who opposed Hasidism, came to be known as *Misnágdim* (literally, "protestants" or "opponents").

In 1802, the Gaon's most prominent pupil, Chaim of Valozhin, set up a new yeshiva in the town of Valozhin (then in the Russian empire's province of Vilna, now in Belarus). It quickly became the mother of Lithuanian yeshivas and inspired the rise of dazzlingly successful new academies in Mir, Telz, Slabodka and other small towns that were to become major "concepts" in Jewish history (and whose derivative yeshivas continue to thrive in the United States and Israel).

One of the best nineteenth-century descriptions of Valozhin (then the Harvard of the world's yeshivas) sums it all up: students felt free to stand on their benches and vigorously contradict what the lecturer was saying, as long as they had a textual, factual basis for doing so.

That defines the Lithuanian way in traditional scholarship: a good student is one who finds grounds to contradict accepted teaching, to bring in new ideas and interpretations. All these Lithuanian Jewish traits were to play a huge role in the secular and modernist movements soon to arise among the ranks of these very Talmudists.

There was, however, one Lithuanian group of Hasidim who sought to combine serious Talmudic scholarship with exuberance in prayer and belief in a hasidic *rebbe:* the group known as Chabad (kha-BAD, itself an acronym for three Hebrew words meaning "wisdom," "understanding," "knowledge"), which has come to be known after its early center in the town of Lubavitch. This is the movement known today for its extensive (and controversial) outreach programs.

By the nineteenth century, Lithuania was home to radical modernist and secularist Jewish movements. The initial impetus may well have come from Berlin and the circle around Moses Mendelssohn who had, in the late eighteenth century, led a bitter campaign against Yiddish, and against distinctive Jewish dress and cultural mores. But the "Berlin Enlightenment" in its original form met with no success in the deeply Jewish, entirely Yiddish-speaking environment of Lita.

What happened will forever be studied as a remarkable case of opposing cultural forces banging into each other and giving rise to a creative third way. Instead of discarding Hebrew and Yiddish in favor of German, Russian, Polish or one of the other majority national languages, East European Jewish cultural leaders, with Lithuania in the forefront, retooled both Yiddish and Hebrew to enable these languages to be used for the most modern of European forms, from the avant-garde novel to the political proclamation. Jewish heritage was being masterfully fused with modern Europe.

The first modern Hebrew poets (among them Adam Hakohen [Odem Hakoyen] and Y. L. Gordon), prose writers (including

Avrom Mapu and Peretz Smolenskin) came from the depths of Jewish Lithuania. Another native of the area was Leyzer Perlman (the later Eliezer ben Yehuda, reviver of modern Hebrew as a spoken vernacular).

The founder of modern Yiddish literature, Mendele Moykher Sforim (the pen name of Sholem-Yankev Abramovitsh, c. 1836–1917), came from Kapulla (Kopyl), also in the depths of *Lita*. His two most prominent early followers, Sholem Aleichem (Sholem Rabinowitz, 1859–1916) and Y. L. Peretz (1852–1915) came from the Ukraine and Poland, respectively. The three, each hailing from a different "third" of Jewish Eastern Europe, made way for a modern Yiddish literature with roots throughout Eastern European Jewry.

Along with modern literature in Hebrew and Yiddish came the revolutionary movements that generally sought to synthesize the radical political and social agenda of the day with the rich internal Jewish culture. The two most prominent movements were Zionism and Jewish Socialism, both of which rose, to a large extent, in *Lita*.

The deep attachment of parts of Lithuanian Jewry to the Land of Israel is often traced to the Gaon's aborted trip there and to the successful migration of a group of his disciples shortly after his death. Many of the founders of East European Zionism, including Peretz Smolenskin and Shmuel Mohiliver, hailed from Lithuania. From about 1907–1914, Vilna was the movement's center. A galaxy of leaders of the State of Israel, from Chaim Weitzman and Zalman Shazar to Shimon Peres, all hail from deep Lithuanian Jewish territory.

One of the prime founders of Jewish Socialism was Aaron Lieberman (1845–80), a native of Luna, a shtetl near Grodna, who joined Aaron Zundelevitsh's circle of young revolutionary Jews in Vilna in the 1870s. After he migrated to London Lieberman issued the first Jewish socialist proclamation. In 1876 he founded the world's first Jewish socialist union, and followed up with a trade union. Both were bitterly condemned by British Jewry establishment that falsely accused the group of having a hidden missionary agenda.

The Jewish Labor Bund was secretly founded in an attic on Antokol Street in Vilna in 1897. Its prime mover was Arkady Kremer (1865–1935), a native of Svintsyan, northeast of Vilna. In the years to follow, its most charismatic leader was Esther Frumkin (1880–c. 1938), a native of Minsk. She became known belovedly simply as "Esther" in Jewish revolutionary circles, and was the first major thinker to unite the Bund's socialism with Yiddishist ideology—the notion of building a modern national minority culture in the everyday language of the people. At the Chernowitz Language Conference of 1908, which proclaimed Yiddish *a* national language of the Jewish people, Esther fought long and hard for the more radical resolution calling for recognition of Yiddish as *the* national language. (She lost.)

The foremost ideologist of the Yiddishist movement (which played a vital role in inspiring the ascent of Yiddish literature to the level of the great European languages) was Chaim Zhitlovsky (1865–1943), a native of Ushatsh, a shtetl near Vitebsk. The small but vibrant foundation that bears his name in New York today continues to publish *Yidishe kultur,* the world's leading Yiddish literary magazine, where David Wolpe's translation into Yiddish of *Lithuania* first appeared.

Marc Chagall heads the list of artists hailing from Jewish Lithuania, but there were scores of others, including Mané Katz, Jacques Lipschitz, and Haim Soutine.

In the period between the two world wars, Jewish Lita found itself divided between three new states, from west to east: independent Lithuania (capital: Kovna, or Kaunas); northeastern Poland (major city: Vilna or Vilno, now Vilnius); the Belorussian Republic of the Soviet Union (capital: Minsk). Like many generalizations the following is flawed, but nonetheless provides an initial orientation to the life of Lithuanian Jewry between the wars. In the two non-Soviet states, traditional Talmudic learning flourished. In the realm of modern secular culture, the Jews in Kovna-centered independent Lithuania tended much more toward Hebrew and Zionism; those in the Vilna region and other parts of the Polish republic leaned much more toward Yiddish, Yiddishism, socialism, and especially Bundism. In the Belorussian republic, in Minsk especially, a major branch of communist Yiddish literature (especially poetry) developed, but was cut down during Stalin's 1937 purge there, which resulted in the murder of the leading authors and cultural figures.

Phenomenally, the old Talmudic genius was rapidly reapplied to modern literature. Even as Talmudic culture continued to thrive, other segments of Lithuanian Jewry were leading the way in creation of most of the major modern Jewish movements, from traditionalist to radical.

The staunch opposition of Lithuanian Jewry to the emotion-based, ecstasy-providing, belief-in-the-rebbe foundations of

Hasidim has been linked in Jewish folklore with the stereotypical image of the Lithuanian Jew, the *litvak.* He or she is meant to be scholarly, serious, dryish, deeply skeptical, emotionally withheld, with an acerbic, piercing, and perhaps self-deprecating humor. The traditional litvak is known for hiding emotions and maintaining outward equanimity in the face of whatever life may present. Among Polish and Ukrainian Jews, the stereotypical litvak, as the great Polish Yiddish writer Y. L. Peretz put it in one of his best-known stories, has "a heart of iron," is somewhat humorless, and above all, lacks the deep unquestioning belief of his southern counterparts. A litvak was disparagingly (but humorously) called a *tseylem-kop* (someone with a cross on their head, in other words, not an unquestioning, utterly devout believer).

Lithuanian Jews speak the famous Lithuanian dialect of Yiddish called *Litvish,* upon which the pronunciation of modern standard Yiddish is based (as is, by the way, the pronunciation of standard Ashkenazic Hebrew).

As in other parts of Jewish Eastern Europe, the central "settlement unit" of Lithuanian Jewish society was the *shtetl,* a townlet or village where Jews formed a significant part of the population. Eastern Europe is full of backwater towns that are insignificant today, but that are famous to Jews worldwide because of pre-Holocaust Jewish civilization.

Myra Sklarew's *Lithuania* focuses in large measure on the Holocaust in Keidan. While commemorating the Holocaust in a given town, it is also important to become acquainted with the town's Jewish history and lore. The following components of that history were gathered by the late Berl Kagan (1911–93) in his magnificent encyclopedia, *Yidishe shtet, shtetlakh un dorfishe yishuvim in Lite* [Jewish Cities, Towns and Villages in Lithuania], (New York, 1990), 465–86.

Keidan's Jewish population dates back to the fourteenth century, when the town was founded. It grew from a fishing village to a townlet. Seventeenth-century documents attest to Jewish activity in the liquor trade. In 1623 the town sent representatives to the Jewish Council of Lithuania and was later to become one of the three main towns in the area of western Lithuania known in Jewish lore as *Zamet*

(Samogitia). Incidentally, there is evidence from old Jewish grave-stones that the town's older Yiddish name was Kadan (ka-DAN).

Keidan suffered a series of calamities in the second half of the seventeenth century, including a ravaging during the Russian-Swedish war in 1655, a plague in 1657, and a massive fire in 1681. The Jews of Keidan were nevertheless known for being relatively well off, and in 1721, their contributions to the Jewish Council of Lithuania topped that of either Vilna or Minsk. The situation worsened considerably after the final partition of Poland in 1795 and the advent of czarist rule.

Various interfaith incidents occurred in Keidan. In 1707, a Christian who claimed that Jews owed him money sealed up the packed synagogue for half a day until he was paid.

That ended peacefully enough. But a century later, in 1809, Menachem Man, the son of Aryeh, was publicly burned as punishment for allegedly having been responsible for convincing the famed Count Pototzky to convert to Judaism.

But in the 1880s, when pogroms were gripping other parts of czarist Russia, the local Christian rulers organized the arrival of a special brigade of Cossacks to *protect* the Jews of Keidan.

Beginning in the early eighteenth century, Keidan was home to a sophisticated yeshiva, where the future Gaon of Vilna studied for a time during his youth. The links between Keidan and the Gaon go even deeper. The rabbis of Keidan had heard about the "boy wonder of Vilna" and in the 1720s rabbi Yehude-Leyb arranged to bring the child for a visit. His "secret" plan was for the already-renowned brilliant lad to one day marry his daughter Chana. And he did.

There are various versions about whether young Eyliohu spent some years in his father-in-law's house in Keidan after marrying Chana (as would have been customary). Nevertheless, his early links with the town and betrothal to one of its daughters are firmly established.

It is also generally accepted that one of the Gaon's early teachers in Keidan was Rabbi Moyshe Margolis, whose tract on the Jerusalem Talmud (completed around 400 A.D. in Palestine) inspired the Gaon in later years to insist on its revived study. (The Babylonian Talmud, completed around 500 A.D. was and is the primary Talmudic standard.) In many of his commentaries, the Gaon demonstrated the absolute necessity of studying the Jerusalem Talmud.

For generations, the rabbis of Keidan were from the famed Katzenelenbogen rabbinic dynasty. Various rabbinic court cases over the centuries centered on whether one or another pretender was a bona-fide Katzenelenbogen. In one case, the ruling was that those who were not genuine would henceforth spell their name with a "p" instead of a "b" to avoid misrepresentation.

One of the best-known rabbis of Keidan was Refoel Yom-tov Halperin. His reputation dates from the tragic period of the "cantonists" (1827 onward), when Czar Nicholas I forced the empire's Jewish communities to supply children for twenty-five years of forced military service (often resulting in bullying aimed at forced conversion). During one Jewish new year holiday, two distraught Jewish women came crying to Rabbi Refoel, reporting that their children had been snatched, apparently "chosen" by the town's rich elite. Rabbi Refoel hastily called the entire elite to the synagogue and threatened to excommunicate all of them if the two boys were not returned within half an hour. They were. (Because of this incident, he ultimately had to leave town, but his courage in standing up to the elite made Keidan famous far and wide.)

The leading reformist Moshe-Leyb Lilenblum (1843–1910) was a native of Keidan. In his earlier career, he argued for religious reform and later on in life became a pioneering Zionist.

Many twentieth-century Hebrew and Yiddish writers, cultural leaders, and teachers hailed from Keidan, among them Isser-Yosef Einhorn, Gershon Keidansky, Aaron Pik, Avrom Shlesinger, and David Wolpe, who continues, in his nineties, to write outstanding Yiddish poetry in Johannesburg.

Between the world wars, the Movshowitz and Cohen printing press in Keidan made the town well known in Lithuanian Jewish booklore. In 1928, they published the brilliant Talmudic commentary of Abraham Isaac Perelman.

The Jews of Keidan enjoyed good relations with their Lithuanian neighbors. In 1909 a circle of Jews convened to help the Lithuanians argue for freedom for Lithuanian culture. A wealthy Lithuanian doctor, Inderavichius, had made it a custom to support one Jewish orphan each year. But these historically good relations did not prevent the massacre that repeated itself in each and every town in Lithuania.

It is true, as David Wolpe writes in his introduction to his translation (originally published in the journal *Yidishe kultur* in New

York), that many in modern-day Lithuania cannot face the truth about the extensive Lithuanian collaboration with the Nazis. But as always, there are exceptions. As fate would have it, one of those exceptions is the courageously truthful Rimantas Zhirgulis, current director of the Municipal Museum in Keidan (now known in Lithuanian as Kedainiai).

In a recent paper on the occasion of the two hundredth anniversary of the death of the Gaon of Vilna, Zhirgulis writes:

> During the twentieth century, the Jews of Kedainiai took part in the struggle for independence along with Lithuanians; they were involved in building an independent Lithuania, and were among those deported to Siberia in June 1941.
>
> As in many other towns in Lithuania, the history of the Kedainiai Jewish community ended tragically; on 28 August 1941, during the Hitlerite occupation, the Germans and their Lithuanian assistants shot dead more than two thousand Kedainiai Jews. That was the end of a community which had lived and been a part of our city for approximately four hundred years. It is our responsibility, as residents of Kedainiai today, to preserve the memory of those who died innocently, and to revive the once rich heritage of the Kedainiai Jewish community; to take pride in the fact that our city was home to the world famous Vilna Gaon, Eyliohu." (Rimantas Zhirgulis, "The Jewish Community of Kedainiai in the 16th-19th C." in I. Lempertas and L. Lempertiene, eds., *The Gaon of Vilnius and the Annals of Jewish Culture,* Vilnius University, 1998, p. 367.)

All the more so is it *our* responsibility, as Jews of East European origin, not only to preserve the memory of the Holocaust, but also to work to preserve and revive the living cultural heritage of our very recent ancestors.

Dovid Katz
Professor of Yiddish Language, Literature and Culture
Vilnius University

Vilnius, January 2000

The Destruction of Keidan

DAVID WOLPE

With the outbreak of the German-Russian war, there emerged in Keidan, as in other parts of Lithuania, the underground Lithuanian fifth column. Fascists and hooligans, realizing that the Nazi beast had broken loose and was on the march across the German-Lithuanian border, began organizing themselves into the notorious Lithuanian "partisan" groups. Preparations were made by them immediately to receive their long-awaited masters from the West. A leading part among the "partisans" was played by the professionals and the "educated"—doctors, chemists, teachers, and government officials, as well as their sons—the high school and university youths and pupils of the local technicum and others. The Keidan "partisans" were headed by two notorious Lithuanians, Povylius and Markunas, both sons of past mayors of the old fascist Lithuanian government. The three Shultchas brothers—Vacys, Juoazs, and Stepas—who lived on the market square, were also leading members of the "partisans" of Keidan. So was Vaclovas Latchinskas, a carpenter on Jasvener Street. All these were particularly active in the murder and plunder of Jews.

The Jews of Keidan sensed that the atmosphere was charged with impending murder and pogrom. The good neighbors of yesterday changed overnight. As time crept on panic began mounting in Jewish homes. No one offered any advice or consolation. The Jews hid in their houses. The young endeavored to flee and reach the Soviet lines in order to enlist in the Russian army. They were shot at by Lithuanians and a number were killed. Others were murdered on the roads by marauding Lithuanians. Only a small number managed to reach the Soviet lines and enlist in the army. Several won distinction in battle, some, such as Izia Gladstein, died heroically on the battlefield. An appreciable number of the fleeing Jews encountered the German army and had no alternative but to return to Keidan. One of them, a gifted Jewish student named Nisan Zaltzburg, in desperation hanged himself in the nearby village of Shat on his return flight.

As soon as the Germans entered Keidan they decreed that all Jews should wear yellow patches. Jews were forbidden to walk on pavements or speak to Lithuanians.

The first organized bloody action by Lithuanians was the rounding up of one hundred Jews, alleged communists. They were marched in their underwear through the village and shot in the Babian (Borer) woods, about two miles from the town. The names known to me of those who were shot are Beno Ronder, Gutman Bloomberg, Jacob Wolpert, Moishe Zalmanowitz with his two daughters Pesse and Bune, Polones the chemist, David Prusak, Avrohom Itche Dinershul, Shmulke, the cab driver (I cannot recollect his surname) and Jonah Shapiro.

A few more episodes of the first days of occupation: Mike Berger, a cinema owner, was beaten so badly by a Lithuanian that he died after being taken to the hospital. Reuven Cessler, a tailor, ran to his parents in "Brom" (at the synagogue yard where fowls used to be slaughtered) and was shot at the gates by a Lithuanian.

A few days later Jews were driven to forced labor. The majority were employed at the airport to unpack bombs left by the Russians. The guards were supplied by the newly formed Lithuanian police. Lithuanian civilians watched from a distance, gloating over the misery of the Jews. Some bombs exploded and about ten Jews were killed.

Other Jews worked in the neighboring government estates, such as Peladnoge (where in the 1920s the first Hachshara farm in Lithuania was established), Podborok, Zherginiai, and others.

Jewish girls were taken to the German officers' club where they were criminally assaulted.

The brutal tortures and murder continued unabated and the Jews lived in constant terror of what the next day might bring.

On 23 July, Lithuanians, with the assistance of a few Germans, loaded some two hundred Jews on six trucks, allegedly to transport them to their labor destinations. After the Jews failed to return, members of their families endeavored to learn of their fates from Lithuanian leaders, but to no avail. A Lithuanian was later bribed with a large sum of money and he brought them the news that on the very same day (23 July) the two hundred were shot in the Tevtshunai woods, ten miles from Keidan. The Jews of Keidan did not want to believe the story and hoped that their nearest and dearest would still return. When a good few days had passed, however, they realized that the news was authentic.

Among these two hundred were: Israel Kahn and his three sons, Zalman, Feivl, and Ortchik, Ortchik Karnowsky who lived near the horse market, the two butcher brothers Yanki and Leizer, together with Leizer's son Bine, the chemist Kagan and his brother-in-law the hardware merchant Pruzhansky, Israel Toiber the baker with his wife and little daughter, Mina Shilkiner who had a stall at the market.

Shortly after this event, the mayor of Keidan, Povylius (who had been reinstated to his former post by the Germans) summoned the leading Jews of Keidan: Zodek Shlapobersky, Chaim Ronder, Chayim Blumberg, Abrasha Kagan, Sroelov, Sholem Chait, and others. Povylius informed them that within twenty-four hours all Jews must leave their homes and move into the vicinity of Smilger Street. Smilger Street together with the synagogue, the synagogue yard and the neighboring alleys up to Langer Street, were fenced off by a barbed wire fence. This became the Ghetto of Keidan.

On the day the Jews moved into the Ghetto, the Lithuanians brought to Keidan all the Jews of the neighboring villages of Shat and Zheim, about a thousand people in all. Among them were also the Jews of other nearby villages who had fled to Shat and Zheim at the outbreak of war. The overcrowding in the Ghetto of Keidan became unbearable. In addition, the food supplies were exhausted. Famine and typhus were imminent.

The mayor imposed a tax on the Jews and threatened extermination unless the required amount became available. The Jews of Keidan gathered all their jewelry and money and gave whatever they could lay their hands on in the hope that this might improve their lot. The hoped-for improvement did not come about. Shortly thereafter the Jews of Keidan were forced on several other occasions to pay taxes.

Some of the youth of Keidan realized the desperate situation and urged leading Jews to flee and hide in the woods or elsewhere. But the community leaders were opposed to such a step, thinking that it would endanger the whole ghetto. They were under the impression that all the Germans wanted was Jewish labor and it was therefore unwise to risk one's life by fleeing.

All illusions ended on 15 August. On that day Lithuanian police and "partisans" under the command of a few Germans drove all Jews from their homes into the synagogue yard. All men over the age of fourteen were marched off four abreast to the huge brick stables of Zhirgynas in the park, which had been a stud farm. The women and children, the old and the ailing, were packed on carts and taken away. Even women with their newborn babies were ordered out of the hospital and brought to the yard. The Lithuanian intelligentsia flocked to witness the spectacle as if it were a circus. Zhirgynas, where the Jewish men were taken, was heavily guarded by Lithuanians. The Jews were kept there for thirteen days. The stables were terribly overcrowded and the Jews received no food at all except for some coffee. The Lithuanians paid the prisoners a few visits and divested them of anything they may still have had left.

When the Jews were driven to the synagogue yard Benzy Birger, a farmer, suggested to a few of the younger ones that they should try and escape past the rivulet Smilge. No one went along with this plan, but he himself fled. For days he hid in the bush. Later, from a hiding place, he witnessed executions of Jews. After the slaughter he went to some peasant friends who hid him. He survived the Nazis and today lives in Keidan.

On Thursday, 28 August 1941, about two hundred Lithuanian railway officials and police assembled at Zhirgynas. All were armed with rifles and hand grenades. First the young and strong Jews were assembled in groups of sixty and taken behind the Catholic cemetery at Datneve Road near the rivulet Smilge. (The Jewish cemetery is higher on a hill above the rivulet.) A huge pit was ready there that had taken Russian prisoners of war five days to dig. The Jews were forced to strip at the mouth of this mass grave and the Lithuanians directed machine guns at them. When the shooting began tractor motors were started in order to silence the shrieks of horror which could be heard even in Keidan. Many wounded fell into this grave and a number who had not been hit were pushed into it and buried alive. This spectacle was watched by prominent members of the Lithuanian society of Keidan, such as the principal of the high school, Selava, mayor Povylius, and a young Catholic priest who also was present.

Rabbi Aaron Galin (the son-in-law of the Rabbi of Keidan, Reb Shlomo Feinsilber), chairman of the Rabbis Association of Lithuania, who was also in Zhirgynas, was among the first group. Standing at the pit he addressed the Jews. He said that the Jewish people had experienced a great many trials. When he cried out that "the innocent blood of those murdered will not remain silent," the shooting commenced.

During the execution there were attempts at fighting back. Among the second group was Zodek Shlapobersky, a man of about forty. He had been an officer in the Lithuanian army and had taken part in the fight for Lithuania's liberation. Shlapobersky had also been a city councilor for many years and was friendly with the Lithuanians. A German officer was in charge of the massacre. Shlapobersky grabbed him, pulled him into the pit, and began strangling him. A Lithuanian with an automatic rifle who stood nearby immediately jumped to the German's assistance. His name was Raudonys and he owned the Hotel Vilnius in the building of the Jewish photographer Joffe. Shlapobersky let the German go, jumped on the Lithuanian, and sank his teeth into the Lithuanian's throat. Shlapobersky was pierced by the bayonets of other Lithuanians and his body was cut to shreds. The gasping Raudonys was immediately taken to hospital where he died two days later. The Lithuanians gave him an imposing funeral. A number of addresses were given in which the Lithuanian bandit was described as "the last victim of Jewish power."

After Shlapobersky's heroic death, the murders became more brutal but also more cautious. The Nazis led smaller groups of Jews to mass graves.

In one of the groups there was the locksmith, Boruch Meir Cessler, the proprietor of a radio and cycle store and locksmith shop. At the pit, he wrenched an automatic pistol from the hands of a Lithuanian, but unfortunately he did not know how to use it. At the same moment two boys fled toward the rivulet but they, as well as Cessler, were shot dead.

The men were followed by women and bigger children, in groups of forty. The bloodthirstiness of the murderers kept increasing. Rashl Shisiansky, the wife of Aba Shisiansky, the miller, pleaded that she be shot first before her children, whereupon the children were wrenched from her and shot before her eyes. Only then did the beasts shoot her. Elderly and ailing women were brought in cars and were buried alive. The small children were thrown in the air by Lithuanians and caught at the point of bayonets.

Lithuanians of Keidan related later that after the pits were covered with a bit of earth the surface heaved up and down as if a live pulse was pulsating in the mass grave, and blood seeped through to the surface. The murderers used rollers to press the earth down in order to arrest the heaving of the bloody earth come alive.

Jews of Keidan who visited the mass grave after liberation stated that the square grave remained higher than the surrounding surface, as if the holy grave wished to [be] separated from the unclean soil that surrounded it.

The shooting of Jews continued until the evening.

Fearing the bitter end that was in store for him, the butcher Hirsh Lebiotkin hanged himself in Zhirgynas.

Of all the Jews who were locked up in Zhirgynas only two escaped by some miracle. One was Chayim Ronder, born in Keidan in 1903, and the other was Shmuel Smolsky. Born in Pausen, Smolsky was a refugee who fled Poland in 1939 and settled in Keidan. Ronder and Smolsky hid themselves behind planks that were lying in Zhirgynas. The clothing of the murdered Jews was brought to Zhirgynas and was guarded. The best items of clothing were plundered by the leaders of the mass murder. The remaining clothes were sorted and later sold cheaply to the Lithuanian population. On the same night of the massacre the two Jews who lay hidden behind the planks and piles of clothing carved a hole in the shingle roof of the stable, took off their boots and lowered themselves on a line made from torn sheets. Luckily they were not seen by the guards and succeeded in reaching the Podborik wood.

Thus; together with the aforementioned Benzy Birger, of the 4,000 martyrs of the three Jewish congregations of Keidan, Shat and Zheim, only three Jews survived.

David Wolpe, translator of Myra Sklarew's Lithuania *into Yiddish, was born in Keidan and survived the horrors of the ghettos and concentration camps, spending a year in Dachau before liberation.*

Preface

MYRA SKLAREW

In 1993, a lifelong dream took on the garments of the possible—travel to the birthplace of my mother's people, Kovno, Lithuania. What I did not know then was that their habitations had once, like the country itself, stretched from the Baltic to the Black Sea, that one could find remnants of our family in literally dozens of towns and villages in Lithuania. Nor could I have known—when I was taken during that first journey to the town of Keidan by one of the few survivors—how important that particular place would become in this quest. Perhaps some will recall that in 1727 R. Avraham Katzenellenbogen brought to Keidan a six-year-old boy from Vilna who had astonished all the rabbis with his talents and abilities. The child later became known as the Gaon R. Eliyahu of Vilna. Here too was the birthplace of Moses Leib Lilienblum, Zionist pioneer. In the twentieth century here in Keidan was born a Yiddish writer, a member of our family, David Wolpe. And it was here, in one day, on the 5th of Elul 5701, that the 500-year-old Jewish community was wiped out.

How can we write about the Holocaust? Adorno speaks of the barbarism in "the so-called artistic representation" of the Shoah. Such representation "contains the power . . . to extract pleasure out of it. . . . Through aesthetic principles of stylization . . . the unimaginable ordeal appears as if it has some meaning; it is transfigured and stripped of some of its horror and this in itself already does an injustice to the victims."

In the long sleepless nights following that first contact with the land so filled with our dead, their voices seemed to well up until it was no longer possible to stay silent. Sometimes, walking out into the night, or in the time of first light when one is vulnerable to sorrow, the words of the poem began to form. As when we bury one we have

31

Meyer Aaron Wolpe (grandfather), born in 1869 in Raseyn, Lithuania (Yasven District, Keidan Region, Kovno Province) holding Anne Wolpe Weisberg, mother of the author, circa 1913. Photo credit: photographer unknown.

loved, when we take the earth into our own hands and place it on the coffin. As Abba Kovner said: "What can we do with you words who have been used in the Holocaust? We take you words onto our lap, we rock you gently, we say 'Don't cry, words, don't cry.'"

David Wolpe had survived the Kovno Ghetto, Dachau, and was alive in South Africa. His son and his family came to visit me, bringing David's books in Yiddish. And I gave David's son my poem about Lithuania and about Keidan where his father had grown up. David was working on the final chapters of his own memoir to be published in Israel and hadn't time to read other works, but one night he awakened sometime before dawn and opened the book I had sent and read the Lithuania poem straight through. And then he began to translate it into Yiddish. A sacred package arrived at my door some months later, tied with black thread—the poem in Yiddish. How to say what that meant to me. And how to tell that when I returned to Lithuania the following year, I brought David's translation and gave it to the Keidan survivor who had taken me walking through Keidan the first time I visited Lithuania. It was as though the circle had been completed.

But perhaps nothing is really completed. One lifetime isn't long enough for that. Only a year ago, after more than sixty years of searching, I found the birthplace of my grandfather—in a tiny hamlet near a river, a place I had circled for five years.

When I buried my father, here in America, I was grateful for his long life, for his life in this country, that he had not had to suffer the loss of trust in the world, that my hopeful father never had to experience what Jean Amery speaks of as being unable to be at home in the world "the accumulated horror . . . blocks the view into a world in which the principle of hope rules."

I am not sorry to have gone to Lithuania. "First and foremost," Michael Steinlauf has written, "there is the powerful, pervasive sense of place. Cities, towns, streets, marketplaces, courtyards, mezuzahs still outlined over doorways; synagogues and cemeteries . . . the Vistula River, cutting through the Polish heartland, whose waters, the writer Sholem Asch once declared, spoke to him in Yiddish; these and countless other sites saturated with the visible and invisible traces of Jewish presence, are all still there, a Jewish geography as yet unmapped, but as real as any. . . . Can we finally accept the challenge of seeing everything, the life as well as the death?"

The Witness Trees

LITHUANIA

1

At three thirty in the morning in America
I have filled an enamel soup pot with cold water
from the sink and I am watering
the apple tree I planted a summer ago,
I am watering the false camelia tree I planted
in March, the crown-of-thorns cactus,
the plant with tiny blue flowers, I am trying
to remember something.

I am trying to remember something I couldn't
possibly know. I am trying,
as I was two days ago in Lithuania,
to move by feel, to know when I was close
to where they had been. At first
I just walked in the Jew's town
without anyone helping me, without anyone
telling me. I walked until I remembered.

But how could I? I had not been here
before. Who could show me
the way? Neither stones
nor saints nor royalty.   Perhaps a man
who bit the throat of a Lithuanian
before they cut him into pieces.   Perhaps
a tiny red poppy I picked from the trench
of the massacre of Keidan—they say the weeds grew

ליטע

• פון
מירא וואָלפע־סקלאַרעוו

ייִדיש:
דוד וואָלפע / יאָהאַנעסבורג

1

האַלב פֿיר אַ זייגער אין דער פֿרי אין אַמעריקע
האָב איך אָנגעפֿילט אַן עמאַלירטן זופטאָפּ מיט קאַלט וואַסער
פֿון דעם וואַשבעקן און כ'האָב זיך גענומען באַוואַסערן
דעם עפּלבוים וואָס איך האָב פֿאַרפֿלאַנצט אַ זומער פֿריִער.
איך באַוואַסער דעם פֿאַלשן קאַמיליע־בוים וואָס כ'האָב פֿאַרפֿלאַנצט
אין מאַרץ, דעם דאָרנקרוין קאַקטוס.
דעם פֿלאַנץ מיט דינע בלאָע בלימעלעך, איך פֿרוּוו
דערמאָנען זיך אין עפּעס.

איך פֿרוּוו זיך דערמאָנען אין עפּעס וואָס כ'קען ניט
אפֿשר עס וויסן, איך פֿרוּוו,
פֿון מײַן זמן מיט צוויי טעג צוריק אין ליטע,
זיך איבערטראָגן מיטן האַרצן, צו דערשפּירן ווי נאָענט כ'בין געווען
ווי זיי זענען געווען. צו ערשט
האָב איך נאָר שפּאַצירט דורך דער ייִדישער שטאָט
אָן עמעצנס הילף, אָן עמעצן
וואָס ווײַזט מיר. כ'בין אַרומגעגאַנגען ביז כ'האָב זיך דערמאָנט.

אָבער ווי האָב איך עס געקענט טאָן? כ'בין דאָך דאָ קיין מאָל ניט געווען
פֿריִער, ווער האָט מיר אָנגעוויזן
דעם וועג? ניט געווען אַ סימן פֿון שטײנער
ניט פֿון די הייליקע און ניט פֿון מלכות, דער ייִד
איז עס געווען וואָס האָט איבערגעגעבן דעם גאָרגל פֿון ליטווינער
איידער זיי האָבן אים צעהאַקט אויף שטיקלעך. אפֿשר
אַ מאָנטשינק קערנדל וואָס כ'האָב אַרויסגעקאָלופּעט פֿון דער טראַנשעע
פֿון דער הריגה אין קיידאַן — מע דערצײלט אַז ס'ווילדגראָז איז געוואַקסן

here twice as tall as anywhere else. How
beautiful it is in Lithuania. See how at Ponar they come
to fetch mushrooms. It was their land long ago. This
was not the only killing they have known. They pick
apples and plums in this season. They pick
cherries. At Ponar they dig for
mushrooms and carry them home
and cook them and eat them—the mycelium

four hundred years in the making nourished
by countless wars, by betrayals, by blood and
bone, by the tears of the dead, by hair and skin. Every
hill is suspect, every ravine, every tree. If you put
your foot down on the earth in Keidan or Datnuva or
Ponar, if you stop walking and read the shape
of the earth under your foot, you can feel the skull
or a bone of someone you knew, someone

you almost remembered. In Kovno a man keeps
the bones of his family from Ponar in a glass
jar on his bookshelf, bones and a bit of earth.
A man keeps a list of the killers. Sometimes
he sends them anonymous letters,
warning them their time has come. Sometimes
he goes further, confronting them directly. He has
nothing more to lose. At his age he endangers

אויף דעם אָרט צוזוי מאָל אַזוי די הייך ווי אומעטום. ווי
שיין עס איז אין ליטע. גיב נאָר אַ קוק ווי זיי קומען אין פֿאַנאַר
קלײבן שוועמלעך. ס'איז זייער לאַנד פֿון גאָר אַ מאָל. דאָס
איז ניט די איינציקע שחיטה וואָס זיי האָבן דורכגעפֿירט. זיי נעמען אַראָפּ
עפּל און פֿלוימען אין דעם סעזאָן. זיי נעמען אַראָפּ
קאָרשן. אין פֿאַנאַר גראָבן זיי אַרויס
שוועמלעך און ברענגען זיי אַהיים
און קאָכן זיי אויס און עסן זיי — מײַצעעליום

פֿיר הונדערט יאָר אויסגעפֿורעמט זיך און גענערט
פֿון אָנצאָליקע מלחמות. דורך פֿאַרדערטעריסקייט, דורך בלוט און
לײַב, דורך די טרערן פֿון די טויטע. דורך בײַן און הויט. איטלעך
בערגל איז חשודיק, איטלעך גראָבן, איטלעך בוים. אויב דו שטעלסט
דײַן פֿוס אַראָפּ אויף דער ערד אין קיידאָן אָדער דאַטנעווע אָדער
פֿאַנאַר, אויב דו שטעלסט זיך אַפּ און באַטראַכטסט די פֿאַרמאָציע
פֿון דעם באָדן אונטער דײַן פֿוס, קענסטו דערפֿילן דעם שאַרבן
אָדער אַ בײן פֿון עמעצן וועמען דו האָסט געקענט, עמעצן

וואָס קומט אָט־אָט צום זכרון. אַ ייִד אין קאָוונע הit־אויף
די בײַנער פֿון זײַן משפחה אין פֿאַנאַר אין אַ גלעזערנעם
סלוי אויף זײַן ביכער־פֿאָליצע, בײנער אין אַ הײפֿל ערד.
אַ ייד אין באַהאַלט אַ רשימה פֿון די רוצחים. אָפֿט מאָל
שיקט ער זיי אַנאָנימע בריוו,
זיי צו וואָרענען אז זייער צײַט איז געקומען. אָפֿט מאָל
טוט ער אַ טריט וויַטער, קאָנפֿראָנטירנדיק זיי דירעקט. ער האָט
ניט מער וואָס צו פֿאַרלירן. אין זײַן עלטער שטעלט ער אין סכנה

only himself.   At Ponar there is a ladder on wheels,
its two parts fold down to the ground. What
is this for? It was used to climb up to the top
of the mound of dead bodies in order to throw
more of the dead onto the pile,
to burn them, to hide the evidence of what
was done here. In Kovno a man keeps a list
of the righteous among the nations. Case by case he documents

acts of kindness and rescue, the names
of those who risked their own lives to save others. Ponar
is a forest, a beautiful forest. The Jews walked
here at night in the dark. Some say they lit candles
to help them see where they were going. Others
say it was fear that showed them the way.
Dante was comforting: in his catalogue
of descents, cause and effect still reigned.

Even he took pity upon Paolo
and Francesca—lovers he treated so tenderly.
But here there was no reason
apart from designation. I name you, tree,
for death. I name you, star, for death, you
grass, you earth, you sister, father. I
name you Christ, I name you Jew name you.
In the territory of the forbidden

like the green ailanthus which dares to grow
in the interstices of stone, they found
what home they could. They occupied air.

40

Ponar: Ladder used for burning exhumed bodies murdered in Ponar Forest.
Photo credit: Myra Sklarew

Ponar Memorial. Photo credit: Myra Sklarew

IX Fort where approximately 40,000 Jews were murdered between 1941 and
1944. Photo credit: Myra Sklarew

Keidan Place of Massacre: 2076 Jews. Photo credit: Myra Sklarew

נאָר זיך אַליין. אין פּאָנאַר איז פֿאַראַן אַ לײַטער אויף רעדלעך.
זײַנע ביידע העלפֿטן לייגן זיך צוזאַמען אויף דער ערד. צו וואָס
האָט מען אים געדאַרפֿט? מע האָט אים גענוצט ארויפֿצוקלעטערן צום שפּיץ
פֿון דער קופּע פֿון טויטע קערפּערס צו קענען ארויפֿווואַרפֿן
מערער מתים אויף דעם הויפֿן,
זיי צו פֿאַרברענען. כדי אויסצובאַהאַלטן דעם עדות־באַװײַז פֿון דאָס
וואָס מען האָט אפּגעטאָן. אַ ייִד אין קאָװנע פֿאַרהיט אַ ליסטע
פֿון די חסידי־אומות־העולם. דאָקומענטירט איינס בײַ איינס

די מעשׂים־טובֿים פֿון חסד און ראַטונקעס, די נעמען
פֿון די וואָס האָבן ריזיקירט מיט זייער אייגן לעבן כדי צו ראַטעווען אַנדערע. פּאָנאר אי
וועלדל, אַ פּראַקטיק וועלדל. ייִדן האָבן
ארומגעשפּאַצירט דאָ אין דעם נאַכט־חושך. מע דערציילט, אַז זיי האָבן אָנגעצונדן ליכ
צו קענען זען ווו זיי גייען. אַנדערע
זאָגן ס'איז געווען דער פּחד וואָס האָט זיי געפֿירט.
דאָנטע האָט נאָך אַ טרייסט: אין זײַן קאַטאַלאָג
פֿון אַראָפֿזינק, רעגירט נאָך אַ סיבה און פּעולה.

אפֿילו ער האָט רחמנות אויף פֿאַאָלאָ
און פֿראַנצישקאַ — ליבהאָבערס וואָס ער האָט אזוי צאַרט באַהאַנדלט.
אָבער אין דעם אָרט דאָ איז ניט געווען קיין סיבה
חוץ פֿון דער באַשטימונג. איך רוף דיר אָן, בוים,
צו טויט. איך רוף דיר אָן, שטערן, צו טויט. דו
גראָז, דו ערד, דו שווועסטער, פֿאָטער. איך
רוף דיר אָן קריסטוס, איך רוף דיר אָן ייִד רוף איך.
אין דעם שטח פֿון די איסורים.

ווי דער גרינער גן־עדן־בוים וואָס וואַקסט מוטיק
אין די שפּאַלטן צווישן שטיינער, האָבן זיי געפֿונען
אַ היים וואָס נאָר ס'האָט זיך געמאַכט. אין דער לופֿטן זיך פֿאַרנומען.

2

As in the days of my father's death when I did
not want to be called back from the opening
through which he was leaving me,
lest I lose sight of him, that if
I turned back to the world, he would be gone
from me forever, I ask my life for silence, for
time, that I may see only the images of Lithuania.
I am trying to remember something. At Passover,

though my Lithuanian grandfather died before I was born,
I always remember him standing
at the head of the table. Strange,
because at Passover we eat reclining.
When the plane hovered over the airfield
in Lithuania just before landing, it looked
like a museum of the ancient wars—helicopters
with wooden propellers like windmills,

World War I airplanes. A strange assortment
of leftovers from various occupations. *Gorbachov!*
explained a man two rows
back. On that first day I walked for miles.
Then I took a tram but couldn't figure
out how to pay. The driver, his body
inserted between glass shields, shrugged
and I shrugged and got off. These are peripheral

ווען אין דער צײַט פון מײַן טאַטנס טויט בעת איך האָב
ניט געוואַלט אויעקגענומען ווערן פון דער עפענונג
דורך וועלכער ער האָט מיך פאַרלאָזן.
טאָמער פאַרליר איך זײַן פנים־אָפּבילד, וואָרעם אויב
כ'וועל זיך צוריק אומדרייען צו דער וועלט, וועט ער שוין זײַן אַוועק
פון מיר אויף אייביק. ווערט מײַן לעבן אַנגעשווויגן ביז צו
דער צײַט, איך זאָל כאַטש קענען אָנקוקן די געשטאַלטן פון ליטע.
איך פרוו זיך עפעס דערמאַנען. בעתן יום־טוב פסח.

הגם מײַן זיידע אין ליטע איז געשטאָרבן איידער כ'בין געבוירן געוואָרן,
האָב איך אים תמיד געדענקט שטייענדיק
אויבן אָן בײַם טיש. מאָדנע,
וואָיל צום פסח־סדר זיצן מיר אַנגעלענט.
ווען דער עראָפּלאַן האָט זיך אַראָפּגעלאָזן איבערן פליפעלד
אין ליטע צו לאַנדן, האָט עס מיר אויסגעזען
ווי אַ מוזיי פון פאַרצײַטיקע מלחמות — העליקאָפּטערס
מיט הילצערנע פּראָפּעלערס אַזוי ווי ווינטמילן.

עראָפּלאַנען פון דער ערשטער וועלט־מלחמה. אַ מאָדנער אָפּקלײַב
פון איבערבלײַבענישן פון פאַרשיידענע אָקופּאַציעס. גאָרבאַטשאָוו!
אַזוי האָט עס דערקלערט אַ מענטש צווי רייען
אַהינטער. אין זעלביקן ערשטן טאָג בין איך זיך אַנגעגאַנגען מײַלן.
נאָך דעם האָב איך גענומען דעם טראַמווײַ אָבער ניט געקענט זיך פונאַנדערקלײַבן
ווי צו באַצאָלן. דער שאָפער, זײַן גוף
אַרײַנגעדריקט צווישן די שופפלאַטן, האָט געקוועטשט מיט די פלייצעס
און איך האָב געקוועטשט מיט די פלייצעס און אויסגעשטיגן. דאָס זענען סתם

notes. I am trying to remember something.
But I stay out of the center
of memory as though it would explode
in my hands if I touched it. I wanted to go there
by feel, to see if Lithuania would tell me
its secrets, to see if I would
recognize myself in Lithuania, to marry the myth
of who I am with the myth of place. To find more

than the signs of the dead. To find evidence
of the lives of those I have come from. Or to give up
Lithuania once and for all. On the airfield
as we landed something was moving
across my field of vision—an old man in a wooden
cart pulled by a horse
as if one century moved through the axis
of another.   Like the wooden house of the last

century wedged between two stone ones. Perhaps
one of my family lived in this house.
How to tell this—like a gospel to say
four versions. Or to say what
is left out. Or to frame the city as the
stage for the drama of salvation,
parables flocking to it
like birds of the air. There is no way

נאַטיצן. איך פּרוּוו זיך עפּעס דערמאַנען.

אָבער איך בין אַרויסגעשלאָגן פֿון דער קאָנצענטראַציע

פֿון זכּרון ווי עס וואָלט האַלטן בײַם אויפֿרײַסן, בײַם אויפֿרײַסן

אין מײַן האַנט אויב כ'וועל דאָס באַרירן. איך האָב געוואָלט אַהין גיין

מיטן אַפּֿילן. און קענענען זען אויב ליטע וועט מיר דערציילן

אירע סודות, צו קענענען זען אויב איך וועל

דערקענען זיך אַליין אין ליטע, זיך צונויפֿקומען מיטן מיטאָס

פֿון וואָר־איך־בין און מיטן מיטאָס פֿון אָרט. אויסגעפֿינען מער

ווי די צייכנס פֿון די טויטע. צו געפֿינען עווידענץ

פֿון די לעבנס פֿון די פֿון וועמען מײַן אָפּשטאַם איז. אָדער מווּתר זײַן

אויפֿן ליטע־צובונד און אויס מיט דעם. אויפֿן פֿליפֿעלד

ווי נאָר געלאַנדט האָט זיך עפּעס באַוועגט

איבער מײַן ווײַזיעפֿעלד — אַ זקן אין אַ הילצערנעם

וואַגן געצויגן פֿון אַ פֿערד

ווי ס'וואָלט זיך אַ יאָרהונדערט מיט דער אַקס צוריקגעדרייט

צום אַנדערן. ווי די הילצערנע קאַטע פֿונעם לעצטן

יאָרהונדערטס אַרײַנגעקלינעוועט צווישן צווײ מויערן. אפֿשר

האָט עמעץ פֿון מײַן משפּחה געלעבט אין דעם הויז.

ווי קען מען עס דערציילן — ווי אַן אמת צו זאָגן

אין פֿיר וואַריאַנטן. אָדער זאָגן וואָס

איז געבליבן אויס. אָדער אײַנרעעמען די שטאָט ווי די

בינע פֿאַר דער דראַמע פֿון גאולה,

די משלים פֿליִען זיך צונויף טשאַטעסוּוַיז צו איר

ווי פֿייגל אין דער לופֿטן. בשום־אופֿן איז ניטאָ ווי

to make the journey to this place. We circle
it, we read it like a map of a district, we name
its alleyways and its houses. We draw in closer
like the camera's eye but we describe
shadows, we describe air fence
lattice petrol cudgel wooden club
water hose gully blood we describe
a man, hardly more than a boy.

He leans on a wooden club, resting—
his murdered lie at his feet his dying
at his feet, his club thick as an arm
high as his chest, he is wearing
a fine suit of clothing his hair
is combed. A group of Jewish men guarded
by armed civilians wait their turn. Within forty-five
minutes the young man has beaten

them to death. And when he is done,
he puts his club to one side
and climbs on the corpses and plays
the Lithuanian national anthem
on his accordian to the clapping
and singing of the nearby civilians—
women hold up their small children to see.
At Keidan in order to cover the cries

צו מאַכן די נסיעה צו אָט דעם אָרט. מיר דרייען זיך אַרום
אים, ווי מיר וואָלטן לייענען די מאַפּע פֿון דעם ראַיאָן. מיר רופֿן אָן
זײַנע געסלעך און זײַערע הײַזער. מיר קומען צו נענטער
ווי די לופֿע פֿון דער קאַמערע אָבער מיר אַנטדעקן
שאָטנס, מיר מערקן צייכנס פֿון אַ לופֿט פֿאַרצאַמונג
אַ פּעטראָל גראָטע, אַ דיקער הילצערנער שטעקן צו ממיתן
אַ וואַסער־קישקע גאָרגל בלוטאָפּפֿאָלוס עס צייכנט זיך אָן
אַ מענטש, קוים מער ווי אַ ייִנגל.

ער שפּאָרט זיך אָן אָן דער הילצערנער בולאָווע, רוט זיך —
זײַנע גערהרגעטע ליגן בײַ זײַנע פֿיס, גוססן
בײַ זײַנע פֿיס, זײַן דראָנג איז גראָב ווי אַן אָרעם
גרייכט אים ביז צו דער ברוסט, ער טראָגט
אַ פֿײַנעם גאַרניטער־אָנטו זײַן האַרפֿריזור
איז פֿאַרקאַמט. אַ גרופֿע ייִדישע מענער באַוואַכט
פֿון באַוואָאָפֿנטע ציוויליסטן ווארטן אויף זײַער ריי. אין פֿינף־און־פֿערציק
מינוט האָט דער יונגער גוי דערשלאָגן

זיי צו טויט. און ווען ער האָט עס פֿאַרענדיקט,
לייגט ער אַוועק זײַן בולאַווע אין אַ זײַט
און קריכט אַרויף אויף די קערפּערס און שפּילט
דעם ליטווישן נאַציאָנאַלן הימען
אויף זײַן אַקאָרדיאָן צום אַפּלאָדיסמענטן־באַגלייט
און מיטזינגען פֿון די אַרומיקע ציוויליסטן —
פֿרויען הייבן אויף זײַערע קליינע קינדער זיי זאָלן עס זען.
אין קיידאָן כדי צו פֿאַרשטילן די קולות

of the Jews forced to strip at the mouth
of a mass grave, the Lithuanians started up their tractor
motors. Those not killed by machine guns were buried
alive. All this was watched by the principal
of the high school, the mayor, and a young
priest. Afterwards, the Lithuanians told that when
the pit was covered with a bit of earth, the surface
heaved up and down as if a live pulse

emanated from that mass grave. In order to stop
the heaving of the blood earth, the Lithuanians
used rollers to press the earth down. The names
of the towns of my family were called Kovno, Volpa,
Keidan, Datnuva, Rasein, Siauliai, Jonava, Pilsiu, Krok.
1939: *Dear Aunt Sara Rivka: Don't be anxious.*
With us things are as they were. We hear about the war
but we don't see it. Russia has just given Vilna

to Lithuania. It is a poor region. We don't know
what will be. We hope for the best. I remember a woman
who sat on the pot where the apples cooked in the cold
basement, her face black from smoke. And here, near this brick
building with a red tile roof, is one of our family, Mausa
Volpe, hatmaker. And nearby, his cousin Aaron. And
here live two killers of Keidan. When I talk to them,
I make them afraid. And here is the hill

פֿון די ייִדן וואָס וועֶרן געצוווּנגען זיך אויסצוטאָן בײַ דער עפֿענונג
פֿון מאַסן־קבֿר, האָבן די ליטווינער געלאָזן אין גאַנג זייעֶרע טראַקטאָר
מאָטאָרן. די וואָס זעֶנען ניט דערהרגעֶט געוואָרן
פֿון די מאַשין־ביקסן האָט מעֶן באַגראָבן
לעֶבעֶדיקערהייט. דאָס אַלץ איז אַבסערוויֶרט געוואָרן פֿון דעֶם דירעֶקטאָר
פֿון דעֶר גימנאַזיע, דעֶם ביֶרגעֶר־מײַסטעֶר און אַ יונגן
גלח. נאָך דעֶם, האָבן די ליטווינער דערצייֵלט אַז וועֶן
די גרוב איז פֿאַרשאָטן געוואָרן מיט אַ ביֶסל עֶרד, האָט די אײַבעֶרפֿלאַך
זיך באַוועֶגט אַרויף און אַראָפּ װי אַ לעֶבעֶדיקער פולס

וואָס הײבט זיך פֿון דעֶם מאַסן־קבֿר. כּדי אָפּצוהאַלטן
דאָס געֶשװילעֶכץ פֿון דעֶר בלוטיֶקער עֶרד, האָבן די ליטווינער
געֶנוצט ראָלוואַלצן אַראָפּצופּרעֶסן דעֶם באָדן. די נעֶמעֶן
פֿון די שטעֶט פֿון מײַן משפּחה זעֶנעֶן געֶװען קאָװנע, װאָלפֿע,
קיֶידאַן, דאַטנאָװע, ראַסיֶין, שאַװל, יאַנאָװע, פֿיֶלז, קראָק.
1939: טמײֶרע טאַנטע שׂרה־רבֿקה: זײַ ניט באַזאָרגט.
אַלץ בײַ מיֶר אונדז איז װי װי געֶװען. מיֶר העֶרן פֿון דעֶר מלחמה
אָבעֶר מיֶר זעֶעֶן זי ניט. רוסלאַנד האָט עֶרשט אַװעֶקגעֶגעֶבן װילנע

צו ליטע. עֶס איז אַן אָרעֶמעֶר קאַנט. מיֶר װייסן ניט
װאָס עֶס קומט. מיֶר האָפֿן אויף דאָס בעֶסטעֶ. איך דערמאָן זיך אַ פֿרוי
װאָס איז געֶזעֶסן איבעֶרן טאַפּ װו די עפּל האָבן זיך געֶקאָכט אינעֶם קאַלטן
קעֶלעֶר, איֶר פּניֶם פֿאַרשװוואַרצט פֿון רויך. און דאָ, בײַ דעֶם ציֶגל
בנין מיֶט אַ רויטן קאַכלדאַך איז געֶװען איֶינעֶר פֿון אונדזעֶר משפּחה, משה
װאָלפֿעֶ, דעֶר היטל־מאַכעֶר. און דעֶרבײַ, זײַן קוזיֶן אהרן, און
דאָ לעֶבן איֶצט צװיֶי רוצחים פֿון קיֶידאַן. וועֶן איך רייֵד מיֶט זײֵ,
װאַרף איך אַן אויף זײֵ אַ מורא. און דאָ איז דאָס באַרגל

49

The Lietukis Garage Massacre: German soldiers and Lithuanian civilians watch Jews being beaten to death by Lithuanian nationalists during the Kovno pogrom, June 26, 1941. Photo credit: Yad Vashem Photo Archives, courtesy of USHMM Photo Archives.

where two sisters ran up and down in order
to lose weight. But they fell ill. And
this is the place where I accidentally killed a kitten—it was
caught in the door. We held a funeral
near the River Nevezis in Keidan. And this is the shop
where Jewish property—after the massacre—was sold
very cheap, three marks for a big bag. The buyer
took his bag to his waiting cart, anxious

to see what he had got: the bag was full of tfillin—
phylacteries used by religious Jews
for prayer. The man didn't know
what these were. Furious, he rode up on the bridge
over the river and threw the tfillin into the water, the dark straps
spreading out like hair in the river.
Here in America, if you rise early enough, in the dark,
if you go out of doors, you can smell autumn

though it is still August. Here and there leaves are beginning
to fall, a few under the dogwood tree, oak leaves, poplar. And just
after dusk, when the earth passes through the dust stream of old
comets, if you look up you will see
meteor showers, the Perseids. Are these burning songs
striking at our atmosphere like the hearts
of those who met their deaths untimely in Lithuania?
I tell you, once we have found our dead, though we cannot hear their

answering voices among the sounds of this world, we will tear
open the skin of the earth
to admit them. We will not lose them again.

ווו צוויי שוועסטער פֿלעגן לויפֿן אַרויף און אַראָפ כּדי
צו פֿאַרלירן וואָג. אָבער זיי זײַנען קראַנק געוואָרן. און
דאָ איז דאָס אָרט וווּ מע האָט ניט ווילנדיק דערהרגעט אַ קעצעלע – עס איז
צעקוועטשט געוואָרן אין אַ טיר. מיר האָבן געמאַכט אַ לוויה
אַראָפ־טײַך פֿון דער נעוואַזשעא אין קיידאַן. און דאָ איז די קראָם
אין וועלכער ייִדיש האָב־און־גוטס – נאָך דער הריגה – איז פֿאַרקויפֿט געוואָרן
גאָר ביליק. דרײַ מאַרק פֿאַר אַ גרויסן זאַק. דער קונה
האָט גענומען דעם זאַק צו זײַן אַפֿואַרטנדיק פֿורל. נײַעגעריק.

צו זען וואָס ער האָט אײַנגעהאַנדלט: ס׳איז געווען אַ פֿולער זאַק מיט תּפֿילין –
תּפֿילין וואָס פֿרומע ייִדן טוען אָן
צום דאַוונען. דער גוי האָט ניט געוווּסט
וואָס דאָס איז אַזוינס. מלא־חמה, האָט ער פֿון בריק
אַרײַנגעוואַרפֿן די תּפֿילין אין וואַסער. די טונקעלע רימענס
האָבן זיך צעצויגן איבערן טײַך ווי די האָר.
דאָ אין אַמעריקע, אויב דו שטייסט אויף גענוג פֿרי, בעת טונקל נאָך,
און גייסט אַרויס אין דרויסן, דערפֿילסטו די האַרבסטלופֿט

כּאַטש עס איז נאָך אויגוסט. דאָ און דאָרט הייבן אָן די בלעטער
אַראָפֿפֿאַלן, אַ ביסל אונטערן קאָרנוס, דעמבבלעטער, פֿאַפֿלאַר. און גלײַך נאָך
בין־השמשות, ווען די ערד יאָגט דורכן שטויבשטראָם פֿון אַלטע קאָמעטן, אויב
דו קוקסט אַרויפֿצו וועסטו זען
מעטעאָר־רעגנס, די פֿערסידס. צי טוט דאָס ברענענדיקע געזאַנג
אַרײַנשלאָגן אין אונדזער אַטמאָספֿער ווי די הערצער
פֿון די וואָס האָבן אַ ליטע באַגעגנט זײַער פֿריצײַטיקן טויט?
איך זאָג, אַז ווי נאָר מיר טרעפֿן זיך מיט אונדזערע מתים, הגם מיר קענען ניט הערן

זייער אָפֿענטפֿער־קול אין וועלטישן געטומל, וועלן מיר אויפֿרײַסן
אָפֿן די הויט פֿון דער ערד
זיי אַרײַנצונעמען. מיר ווילן זיי מער ניט פֿאַרלירן.

3

But is this the way their story will end?
Not this way. Not yet.
For here is the place where the young brother
was killed, his wife, the infant nearly ready
to enter this world. In the fire that burned
the mother alive, the baby exploded from her
belly like the sacred letters of the scroll
Akiba was wrapped in when the Romans

set him afire. Wedged between the life
before life and the life to come, for a single
moment the child looked upon this world
before it too entered the flames. An old woman—
her face so close I hear her labored
breathing, I smell her skin—thinks we are
survivors come back, pierces the silence with a voice
so calamitous, tells us about her neighbor

who escaped from the pit in Krakiai
where all others were murdered. He went
to the people to whom he had entrusted his
property, but they betrayed him, sending
him back to his death. Is she one of the righteous
or one who is haunted by the past? Or one
who fears the survivor who will turn up
one day at her door and ask for his house

אָבער צי זאָל זיך זייער געשיכטע ענדיקן אויף דעם אופֿן?
ניט אויף דעם אופֿן. נאָך אַלץ ניט אַזוי.
וואָרעם דאָ איז דער אָרט וווּ דער יונגער ברודער
איז דערהרגעט געוואָרן, זײַן ווײַב, דאָס עופֿעלע קימעט צמייטיק
צו קומען אויף דער וועלט, אין פֿמער וואָס האָט פֿאַרברענט
לעבעדיקערהייט די מאמען. האָט דער עמבריאָן אַרויסגעפֿלאַצט פֿון איר
ווי די הייליקע אותיות פֿון דער תּורה
אין וועלכער די רוימער האָבן אַנגעוויקלט רבי עקיבא

און אים אַרויפֿגעלייגט אויפֿן שמטער. אַרנגעשפּאַרט צווישן לעבן
פֿאַר דעם לעבן און נאָך דעם לעבן, פֿאַר אַן איינציקער
רגע האָט דאָס קינד געכאַפּט אַ בליק אויף דער וועלט
איידער אויך ער איז פֿאַרצוקט געוואָרן פֿון די פֿלאַמען. אַן אַלטע פֿרוי —
איר פּנים אַזוי נאָענט אַז איך פֿיל איר יסורימדיק
אָטעמען, איך דערשמעק איר הויט — זי מיינט מיר זענען
לעבן־געבליבענע, איר קול שטעכט דורך די שטילקייט
אַזוי אומגליקלעך, זי דערצײַלט אונדז פֿון איר שכן

וואָס איז אַנטלאָפֿן פֿון דער גרוב אין קראָק
וווּ מע האָט אַלעמען אויסגעמאָרדעט. ער איז געגאַנגען
צו די מענטשן וועמען ער האָט אָנגעטרויט זײַן
פֿאַרמאָג, נאָר זיי האָבן אים פֿאַרראַטן, טרבנדיק
אים צוריק צום טויט. איז אָט די יינע פֿון די רעכטפֿאַרטיקע
אָדער איינע וואָס ווערט געמוטשעט פֿון דעם עבֿר? אָדער אזאַ
וואָס האָט מורא אַז אַ לעבן געבליבענער וועט זיך באָווזן
איין טאָג בײַ איר טיר און פֿאָדערן זײַן הויז

back, ask for a place to breathe again, ask
what has become of his small son?
They cut off the head of the rabbi
of this town and set it in the window. Was he
to be a talisman, keeping watch over
them like a ship's figurehead sighting
the dangers before them? Or an object
of ridicule? Or by fixing his head

like a beacon light in their window, they could hold
imprisoned the heart of his people? What hatred, what
fear carries human action to this place?

צוריקגעבן, וועט ווידער זוכן א פלאַץ ווו צו קענען אָטעמען, וועט פֿרעגן
וואָס איז געוואָרן מיט זײַן זונעלע?
זיי האָבן אָפּגעשניטן דעם רבֿס קאָפּ
פֿון דער זעלביקער שטאָט און אים אַרײַנגעשטעלט אין פֿענצטער. האָט ער
עס געדאַרפֿט זײַן פֿאַר זיי א קמיע, פֿאַרהיטן און באַשיצן
זיי ווי די שיף־פּאָפּקע וואָס קוקט אויס
די סכּנות פֿאַרויס פֿון זיי? אָדער גאָר א זאַך
פֿון חוזק? אָדער בײַם אַרויסשטעלן זײַן קאָפּ

ווי שײַנטורעם־ליכט אין זייער פֿענצטער. וועלן זיי קענען האַלטן
געפֿאַנגען דאָס האַרץ פֿון זײַן פֿאָלק? וואָס פֿאַר א שׂינאה, וואָס
דער פחד טראָגט מענטשלעכע מעשׂים צו דעם אָרט?

This then is the story of my people, the story of what
became of my family—those who had not come away
earlier, those who survived the pogroms
after the assassination of Czar Alexander II. At Keidan
after the massacre of 2000 Jews
one escaped who afterwards hid in the forest
in a bunker. Through the night and in early
morning kind villagers brought him food.

The head of the village discovered some coming
with food and offered 10,000 marks' reward for the man
dead or alive. He invited the police. Twenty of them
circled the bunker dug into the earth, a small chimney
for fresh air. They issued an ultimatum to come out
or they would set off explosives deep in the earth.
The man, half asleep, thinking he was already dead,
arose, wearing one shoe and carrying two grenades.

Pretending to surrender, he attempted to explode
the first grenade but had forgotten to put off
the ring. He fell back to the earth, repeating the episode
with the grenade, this time exploding it. Some were
killed, some wounded. Till they got their consciousness
back, he escaped. He came to the house of
villagers. What happened after, what I want
to tell—they put him on the oven, he had fallen sick

דאָס איז די געשיכטע פֿון מײַן פֿאָלק, די געשיכטע פֿון וואָס
איז געוואָרן פֿון מײַן משפּחה — די וואָס זענען ניט אַוועק
פֿרײַער. די וואָס האָבן איבערגעלעבט די פֿאָרגראַמען
נאָך דעם אַטענטאַט אויף צאַר אַלעקסאַנדער דעם צווייטן אין קיִיעוואַן
נאָך דער רציחה פֿון צוויי טויזנט יִדן
איז איינער אַנטלאָפֿן און נאָך דעם זיך אויסבאַהאַלטן אין וואַלד
אין אַ בונקער. דורך דער נאַכט און פֿרי
באַגינען פֿלעגן גוטע פּויערים אים ברענגען שפּײַז.

דער דאָרף־עלטסטער האָט דערשמעקט אַז מע טראָגט אַהין
עסנוואַרג און ער האָט אָנגעבאָטן 10,000 מאַרק באַלוינונג פֿאַר דעם יִדן
טויט אָדער לעבעדיק. ער האָט געבראַכט פֿאַליציי. צוואַנציק פֿון זיי
האָבן אַרומגערינגלט דעם אין דער ערד אויסגעגראַבענעם בונקער, מיט אַ קוימענדל
אויף פֿרישער לופֿט. זיי האָבן אַרויסגעגעבן אַן אולטימאַטום אַרויסצוקומען
אָדער זיי וועלן אַרײַנלייגן טיף אין דער ערד אויפֿרײַס־מאַטעריאַל.
דער יִד, האַלב שלעפֿעריק, וויסנדיק אַז ס'איז שוין זײַן טויט,
האָט זיך אויפֿגעהויבן, אָנגעטאָן איין שוך און האַלטנדיק צוויי גראַנאַטן,

מאַכנדיק דעם אָנשטעל אַז ער גיט זיך איבער האָט ער געפֿרוווט אויפֿרײַסן
דעם ערשטן גראַנאַט אָבער ער האָט פֿאַרגעסן אַראָפּצונעמען
דעם רינג. ער האָט ווידער אַ פֿאַל געטאָן צו דער ערד, איבערהזרנדיק די טוווּנג
מיטן גראַנאַט, דאָס מאָל האָט עס עקספּלאָדירט. עטלעכע זענען
אומגעקומען, עטלעכע פֿאַוווּנדט. ביז זיי זענען צו זיך געקומען
ווידער, האָט ער געמאַכט אַ בראַך. ער איז אָנגעקומען צו אַ הויז
פֿון פּויערים. וואָס נאָך דעם האָט פּאַסירט, איז דאָס וואָס כ'וויל
דערצײַלן — זיי האָבן אים געמאַכט אַ געלעגער אויפֿן אויוון, ער איז געוואָרן קראַנק

from the cold and the snow and suddenly he saw
on the peasants' hut parchment of the Torah glued
to the walls. He knew them to be good people but
he was frightened and escaped from the oven: "I must
go," he insisted. Later he came back, he found
the Torah had been cut from the walls and replaced
with newspapers. Those who lived in the house
had understood why he had run away from them.

After the War, he considered the day of his escape
from the bunker as his second birth
and on that day each year he fasted.
Here is the house of Yankele Gross—Pasmilga 2.
We would close the windows on Easter
when they came from St. George's Church.
They would start to drink. You never knew
what would happen. And here is the house

where the wife spent all their money
on shopping. But it was not allowed for a Jew
to go hungry on the Sabbath. All the families
would raise funds for food. And here
is the house with the thatched roof. When the
goat got hungry we would take straw
from the roof. And here is where the chief
of the firemen lived, Zodek, who dared

פֿון דער קעלט און שניי נאָר פּלוצלינג האָט ער דערזען
אין דער פֿיעִרישער כאַלופּע פֿאַרמעטן פֿון דער תּורה אַרויפֿגעקלעפּט
אויף די וואָנט. ער האָט זיי געקענט ווי גוטע מענטשן אָבער
ס׳איז אים באַפֿאַלן אַ פּחד און ער איז פֿון זיי אַנטלאָפֿן: „איך מוז
אַוועקגיין", האָט ער זיך אַוועגעשפּאָרט. שפּעטער איז ער צוריקגעקומען, ער האָט דער
די תּורה-יריעות זענען גענען פֿון די וואָנט אראָפּגענומען און פֿאַרביטן
מיט צײַטונג-פּאַפּיר. די וואָס האָבן אין הויז געוווינט
האָבן פֿאַרשטאַנען פֿאַר וואָס ער איז פֿון זיי אַנטלאָפֿן.

נאָך דער מלחמה, האָט ער אָנגענומען דעם טאָג פֿון זײַן אַנטלויפֿן
פֿון בונקער ווי זײַן צוווייטן געבוירן ווערן
און אין דעם טאָג האָט ער איטלעך יאָר געפֿאַסט.
דאָ איז דאָס הויז פֿון יאַנקעלע גראָס — פֿאַסמילגאַ 2.
מיר פֿלעגן פֿאַרמאַכן די פֿענצטער אין פֿאַסקאַ
ווען זיי פֿלעגן צוריקקומען פֿון סאַנט דזשאַרדזש קלויסטער.
זיי פֿלעגן אָנהייבן שיכורן האָסטו קיין מאָל ניט געוווּסט
וואָס עס קען פֿאַסירן. און דאָ איז דאָס הויז

ווו דאָס ווײַב האָט אויסגעגעבן גאָר זייער געלט
אויף אַנקויף. אָבער אַ ייִד האָט ניט געטאָרט
בלײַבן הונגעריק אום שבת. אַלע משפּחות
פֿלעגן צוזאַמענקלײַבן געלט אויף עסן. און דאָ
איז דאָס הויז מיטן שטרוייענעם דאַך. ווען די
ציג איז הונגעריק געוואָרן פֿלעגן מיר נעמען שטרוי
פֿון דעם דאַך. און דאָ איז ווו דער נאַטשאַלניק
פֿון דער פּאָזשאַרנע-קאָמאַנדע, צדוק, האָט געוווינט, ער האָט מוטיק

to resist the murders and was brutally killed.
And here Rifka, beautiful but meshugah. In winter,
normal; in summer she would go naked
through the streets. And here the Bet Midrash
with the big arch on top and the sundial with Hebrew
letters: Yud Aleph, Yud Bet. And here we
joke with the women who have come
out to the fence to talk with us: Perhaps we

will take back your house. Startled, they laugh. And here
is the cheder lived in by a peasant and soon
to be destroyed. And here a long wooden
house where Moshe Leib Lilienblum was
born. It was also a tea house. You had to bring
your own sugar. In the bottom of this house
I was born, a man tells me. What was it like
getting born in this house? I don't remember.

But I know for certain I was born naked.
The youngest of eight children. Two weeks later my father
died of tuberculosis. And my mother lost her milk. I was nursed
by a wet nurse. I have a milk brother in Israel.
And here we used to eat mice. The purpose of a piece
of bread was to catch a mouse. Now one of the mouse eaters
is a pilot in the Israeli air force. Not poor, not rich, not drunk-
ards— earth, a cow, a few cucumbers. One brother twenty-one

years old was as a father for me. All to the left
of Smilgos Street was the Ghetto. The Smilga River:
old Jewish cemetery on one shore; mass grave on the other.

זיך אַנטקעגנגעשטעלט די רוצחים און איז בעסטיאַליש דערהרגעט געוואָרן.
און דאָ רבֿקה, אַ משוגענע קראַסאַוויצע, אום ווינטער,
נאָרמאַל; אין זומער פֿלעגט זי אַרומגיין נאַקעט
אין די גאַסן. און דאָ איז דער בית־מדרש
מיטן גרויסן בויגן אין דער הייך און דער זונזייגער מיט העברעישע
אותיות: יאָ, יבֿ. און דאָ פֿלעגן מיר זיך אונטערהאַלטן
שפּאַסיק מיט די ווײַבער וואָס פֿלעגן אַרויסקומען
צום צוים אויף אַ שמועס מיט אונדז: אפֿשר

וועלן מיר נעמען צוריק דעם הויז. אויפֿגעשראָקן, פֿלעגן זיי לאַכן. און דאָ
איז דער חדר וווּ ס׳לעבט אַ פֿייער און בקרובֿ
וועט מען אים אַרונטעררײַסן. און אין דעם לאָנגן הילצערנעם
הויז איז משה לייב לילִיענבלום געבוירן
געוואָרן. ס׳איז דאָ אויך געווען אַ טשטַנע. פֿלעגסט מוזן ברענגען
דײַן אייגענעם צוקער. אונטן אין דעם הויז
בין איך געבוירן געוואָרן, דערצײַלט מיר אַ ייִד. ווי פֿילט מען זיך
וווּרנדיק געבוירן אין דעם הויז? איך געדענק ניט,

נאָר אַיין זאַך ווייס איך אויף זיכער כ׳בין געבוירן געוואָרן נאַקעט.
דער יינגסטער פֿון אַכט קינדער. צוויי וואָכן שפּעטער איז מײַן טאַטע
געשטאָרבן פֿון טובערקולאָז. און מײַן מאַמע האָט
פֿאַרלאָרן איר מילך געזויגן האָט מיר
אַ ניאַניע. איך האָב אַ מילך־ברודער אין ישראל.
און דאָ פֿלעגן מיר עסן מײַז. דער ציל פֿון אַ ברעקל
ברויט איז געווען צו כאַפֿן אַ מויז. איצט איז אַיינער פֿון די מײַז־עסערס
אַ פֿילאָט אין ישׂראלס לופֿטפֿלאָט. ניט אָרעם, ניט רײַך, ניט קיין שיכורים —
עֶרד, אַ קו, עטלעכע אוגערקעס. אַ ברודער פֿון אַיין־און־צוואַנציק

יאָר אַלט איז געווען ווי אַ טאַטע צו מיר. אַלץ אויף דער לינקער
זײַט פֿון סמילגער גאַס איז געווען די גאַטאָ. דאָס סמילגע טײַכל:
דער אַלטער ייִדישער בית־עולם אויף אַיין ברעג; דער מאַסן־קבֿר אויפֿן אַנדערן.

In Vilnius, outside my window, three boys throw
broken glass bottles at one another. Now the glass
shatters against the building, now it showers down
on the victim. Sometimes the thrower trips
on the garbage or debris of building materials. One
is the target; the others the shooters. Then the game
changes: everyone for himself. At first I peer
from a corner of the window. Then I stand framed

in the window so they can see me. The sounds
of broken glass, their high-pitched shouts
cease. At Ponar, while they dug up the bodies
for burning, a few of the Jews dug a tunnel from the pit that
they might escape into the forest. But along
its entire route, the tunnel had been mined. My mother
loved the small pears just come into season,
like those on the table of the old ones in Datnuva.

My Lithuanian grandmother preserved cherries,
removing the stones with a hairpin and a cork. On
the table in Datnuva are quart jars of cherries. Chaya
brings me a bag of small pears to take to America
but I leave them for one who will come here
after me. In Lithuania we are under the ozone hole,
fearful of the sun. A man tells me, Here, a big hole was dug.
They were looking for gold, gold teeth, gold

אין ווילנע, הינטער מײַן פֿענצטער וואַרפֿן דרײַ ייִנגלעך
צעבראָכענע פֿלעשער אײנער אױפֿן אַנדערן. אָט ווערט דאָס גלאָז
צעשמעטערט אױפֿן בײן, אָט שפּריצט זיך עס פֿונאַנדער
אױף אַ שפּיל־קרבן. צו מאָל טרעט דער וואַרפֿער אַרױף
אױף בראָכוואַרג צי מיסט פֿון בױ־מאַטעריאַלן. אײנע
זענען דער ציל; די אַנדערע די שיסערס. נאָך דעם ווערט די שפּיל
געביטן: יעדער אײנער פֿאַר זיך, צו ערשט קוק איך
פֿון אַ ווינקל בײַם פֿענצטער. נאָך דעם שטײ איך אַװעגערעמט

אין פֿענצטער זײ זאָלן מיך קענען זען. די קלאַנגען
פֿון צעבראָכן גלאָז, זײערע הױך־צעשריגענע קולות
הערן אױף. אין פֿאַנאָר, בעתן אױפֿגראַבן די קערפּערס
צו פֿאַרברענען, האָבן אַ ביסל ייִדן געגראָבן פֿון דער גרוב אַ טונעל אַז
זײ זאָלן קענען אַנטלױפֿן אין דעם וואַלד. אָבער אױס לענג
דעם גאַנצן וועג, איז דער טונעל געוווען מיניערט. מײַן מאַמע
האָט האַלט געהאַט קלײנע בערנעלעך וואָס זענען געקומען אין סעזאָן,
ווי די אױפֿן טיש פֿון די אַלטע לײַט אין דאַטנעװוע.

מײַן באַבע פֿון ליטע האָט געפֿערגלט קאָרשן,
אַרױסנעמענדיק די בײַנדלעך מיט אַ האַרשפּילקע אױף אַ קאָריק. אױפֿן
טיש אין דאַטנעווע זענען געוווען קוואַרט־סלױעס מיט קאָרשן. חיה
ברענגט מיר אַ זעקל מיט קלײנע בערנעלעך מיטצונעמען קײן אַמעריקע
נאָר איך לאָז זײ זײ איבער פֿאַר די וואָס וועט קומען אַהער
נאָך מיר. אין ליטע זענען מיר אונטער דער אַזאַן־לאָד,
אין מורא פֿאַר דער זון, אַ מענטש דערצײַלט מיר, דאָ, איז אַ גרױסע לאָך
אױסגעגראָבן,
זײ האָבן געזוכט גאָלד, גאָלדענע צײַנער, גאָלדענע

wedding rings, rummaging among the bones
of the dead. Ten years ago I found a black scalp
with hair. I was sure it was my father's brother.
After the killing this was a bald field. They grew up
by themselves, these trees. We understood
because here these weeds were higher, twice,
than the others. August 28, 1941: The local
collaborators under the SS killed two thousand and

seventy-six people. The local chief doctor
supervised the process. The first group
of one hundred people—elderly, the sick—brought
here, alive. Among them, my mother. Zodek
saw the first group ordered to take off their clothing.
Two men refused. Zodek grabbed a pistol from the hand
of the killer, shot him in the back. The doctor
couldn't help the killer. Two hours later he

died in the hospital. On the third day, his funeral.
One thousand people came. On his tombstone,
it was written: This man died through his duty.
Zodek threw into the pit one German commandant,
jumped with him into the pit and was hit with a pistol,
his teeth in his throat. The other Lithuanian jumped
into the pit. He used a knife to cut Zodek and saved
the commandant. And one more incident: One Jew

קידושין רינגען, נישטערנדיק דורך די ביינער
פֿון די מתים. מיט צען יאָר צוריק האָב איך געפֿונען אַ שוואַרצן שאַרבן
מיט האָר. איך בין געווען זיכער עס איז מײַן טאַטנס ברודער.
נאָך דער הריגה איז עס עס געבליבן אַ נאַקעט פֿעלד. דאָ איז אַלץ געוואַקסן
פֿון זיך אַליין, אָט די ביימער, מיר האָבן פֿאַרשטאַנען
פֿאַר וואָס דאָס ווילדגראָז איז דאָ העכער, צווי מאָל אַזוי הײך,
ווי די אַנדערע. אויגוסט 28, 1941: די היגע
קאָלאַבאַראַטאָרן מיט די עסעס האָבן אויסגעהרגעט צווי טויזנט און

זעקס־און־זיבעציק ייִדן. דער היגער שעף־דאָקטער
האָט אויפֿגעפֿאַסט דעם גאַנג. די ערשטע גרופּע
פֿון הונדערט מענטשן — אַלטע, קראַנקע — זענען געבראַכט געוואָרן
אַהער, לעבעדיקע. צווישן זיי, מײַן מאַמע. צדוק
האָט געזען ווי מע באַפֿעלט די ערשטע גרופּע זיך אויסצוטאָן,
צוויי מענטשן האָבן זיך אָפּגעזאָגט. צדוק האָט אַרויסגעכאַפּט אַ רעוואָלווער פֿון האַנ‌ט
פֿון אַ רוצח, ער האָט אים אַרײַנגעשאָסן אין רוקן. דער דאָקטער
האָט דעם מערדער ניט געקענט העלפֿן. צווי שעה שפּעטער איז ער

געשטאָרבן אין שפּיטאָל. אויפֿן דריטן טאָג, איז געווען זײַן לוויה,
טויזנט מענטשן זענען געקומען, אויף זײַן מצבֿה,
איז אויפֿגעשריבן: דער מאַן איז געשטאָרבן בעתן דערפֿילן זײַן פֿליכט.
צדוק האָט אַרײַנגעוואָרפֿן אין גרוב אַ דײַטשישן קאָמענדאַנט,
אַרײַנגעשפּרונגען מיט אים אין גרוב און געגעבן אַ זעץ מיט אַ פֿיסטויל
אַרײַנגעקלאַפּט די צײן אין גאָרגל. אַ ליטווינער איז אַרײַנגעשפּרונגען
אין גרוב. ער האָט אַרײַנגעשטאָכן אַ מעסער אין צדוקן און גערעטעוועט
דעם קאָמענדאַנט. און נאָך אַן אינצידענט: אַ ייִד

had hidden a knife and he beat one collaborator
he knew who was brought
to the hospital. He told the doctor he wanted
to participate in the Jewish killing and came back.
After the War the death sentence was banned.
The murderer was sentenced to 15 years.
He spent 12 years in prison; later he lived near Datnuva
until his natural death. Vacationing

school pupils used to participate in the killings. The doctor was
brought to trial not because of his experiences in the War
but as a thief, sentenced to five years.

האָט באהאַלטן אַ מעסער און האָט אים אַרײַנגעהאַקט אין אַ קאָלאַבאָראַטאָר
וואָס ער האָט אים געקענט. ער איז געבראַכט געוואָרן
אין שפּיטאָל. ער האָט דערצײַלט דעם דאָקטער אַז ער האָט געוואָלט
זיך באַטייליקן אין דעם יִדישן אויסראָט און קומען צוריק.
נאָך דער מלחמה האָט מען בטל געמאַכט טויטשטראָף,
דער רוצח איז פֿאַרמישפּט געוואָרן אויף 15 יאָר,
ער איז אין טורמע געזעסן 12 יאָר; נאָך דעם האָט ער געווינט בײַ דאַטנעוווע
ביז זײַן נאַטירלעכן טויט. בעת וואַקאַציעס

פֿלעגן שילער זיך באַטייליקן אין די הריגות. דער דאָקטער איז
געבראַכט געוואָרן צו אַ מישפּט ניט מחמת זײַנע מעשים בעת דער מלחמה
נאָר ווי אַ גנב, פֿאַרמישפּט אויף פֿינף יאָר.

69

Be wary of old forts—they have a history
of killing; their walls are used to the screams
of prisoners, the silence of death. Their walls
are impervious to the last messages
scrawled in blood. There is no poetry in any
of this. These forts have witnessed
the deaths of over 100,000 Jews. Be wary
of names. Those who took the long

road from ordinary life to the ghetto and
from the ghetto to the Ninth Fort called that way
Via Dolorosa—Christ's walk
to Golgotha. The road that led uphill from
Kovno to the Ninth Fort. The Germans called it
the Way to Heaven—*Der Weg*
zur Himmel-Fahrt. And in secret they named it
Place of Extermination No 2, *Vernichtungstelle nr. 2.*

Not existing place, *vernichtungstelle.* No,
that's not quite it. A transitive word, more active—
place to make nothing, to nullify, cancel, annul.
You must say these names yourself. Taste
the strange mixtures of annihilation, the Jew
using Christian iconography, going in columns
of a hundred along the sorrowful way.
In the Ninth Fort the power went off.   We

זײ געוואָרנט פֿאַר אַלטע פֿאָרטן — זיי האָבן זייער געשיכטע
פֿון הריגה; זייערע וועגנט זענען געווינט צו די גוואַלדן
פֿון געפֿאַנגענע, צו דער שטילקייט פֿון טויט. זייערע וועגנט
בלײַבן קאַלט צו די לעצטע אָנזאָגן
אַנגעפֿינטלט מיט בלוט. ניטאָ קיין פֿאַעזיע אין קיין איינעם
פֿון אָט די, די פֿאָרטן זענען עדות
פֿון דעם טויט פֿון מער ווי הונדערט טויזנט ייִדן, זײ געהיט
מיט נעמען. די וואָס זענען געגאַנגען דעם לאַנגן

וועג פֿון אַ פּשוט לעבן ביז צו דער געטאָ און
פֿון געטאָ צום נײַנטן פֿאָרט מיינט דער וועג
ווײַ דאָלאָראָזאַ — דער גאַנג פֿון קריסטוסן
צו גלגלתא. דער וועג וואָס פֿירט באָרג-אַרויף פֿון
קאָוונע צום נײַנטן פֿאָרט. די דײַטשן האָבן אים גערופֿן
דער וועג צום הימל — דער וועג
צור היממעל-פֿאָהרט. און בסוד האָבן זיי עס גערופֿן
פּלאַץ פֿון עקסטערמינאַציע נומ. 2. פֿערניכטונגסשטעללע נר. 2.

אַ ניט עקסיסטירנדיק אָרט, פֿערניכטונגסשטעללע. ניין,
דאָס איז ניט אין גאַנצן גענוי. אַ טראַנסיטיוו וואָרט, מער אַקטיוו —
אַ פּלאַץ וואו מע מאַכט אויס, מע אַנולירט, מע מאַכט בטל, ליקווידאַציע.
דו מוזט די נעמען פֿאַר זיך אַליין איבערטראַכטן, דערפֿילן דעם טעם
פֿון די משונהדיקע גערמישן פֿאַרניכטונג, דער ייד
נוצנדיק קריסטלעכן איקאָנאָגראַפֿישן סימבאָליזם, גייט אין רייען
פֿון הונדערט מיט דעם פֿײַנדלן וועג.
אין נײַנטן פֿאָרט איז דער כּוח אויסגעגאַנגען. מיר

stood in the cold dark, in the cold, in the
dark. We could smell the air they had breathed.
I wanted, above all, to escape.   But I kept
my feet on the ground. We lighted candles
and we walked through the steel blackness.
The woman with me had worked there twelve years.
Her face had no expression as she talked about what
happened there, the voice drilling into my head.

In the barracks, dug deep into the ground, heavy
steel doors. Deep trenches surrounding the
fortifications. High concrete walls, rows of barbed
wire. Trucks whose motors were run to drown
out the sound of crying, of shooting. Guards
who beat and chased them into the path of the guns
of the Lithuanian partisans. *October 4: Kovno, 9th fort—*
315 Jewish men, 712 Jewish women,

818 Jewish children (punitive action because
a German policeman was shot at in the ghetto). October 29:
Kovno, 9th fort—2,007 Jewish men, 2,920 Jewish women,
4,273 Jewish children (removal from the ghetto of surplus Jews).
Digging and burning. What was
buried had to be unburied. The Master of Fire,
the expert on burning supervised the firemen,
three hundred bodies exhumed and burned

each day until the flour of dead souls disappeared
in the earth or fled upward into the air.

זענען געשטאַנען אין דער קאַלטער פֿינצטערניש, אין דער קרירה, אין דעם
חושך. מיר האָבן געפֿילט די לופֿט וואָס זיי האָבן געאָטעמט.
איך האָב געוואָלט, מער ווי אַלץ, אַנטלויפֿן. אָבער כ׳האָב זיך אַנגעהאַלטן
ניט אַוועקצוגיין פֿון דעם אָרט. מיר האָבן אָנגעצונדן ליכט
און מיר זענען געגאַנגען דורך דער שטאָק־פֿינצטערניש.
די פֿרוי בײַ מײַן זײַט האָט דאָ געאַרבעט צוועלף יאָר.
איר פנים איז געווען אָן אויסדרוק ווען זי האָט דערציילט וועגן דעם
וואָס עס האָט דאָ פֿאַסירט. איר קול האָט מיר געבויערט דורכן קאָפּ.

אין די באַראַקן, פֿאַרגראָבן טיף אין דער ערד, זענען שווערע
שטאָלענע טירן. טיפֿע טראַנשעען רינגלען אַרום די
פֿאַרטיפֿיקאַציעס. הויכע בעטאָנענע ווענט, רייען פֿון שטעכל־
דראָט. משׂא־אויטאָס וואָס זייערע מאָטאָרן האָבן געאַרבעט צו פֿאַרשטומען
די יאָמער־געשרייען, דאָס שיסערײַ. וואַכפּאָסטנס
וואָס האָבן געשלאָגן און אַרומגעיאָגט אין ציל־סטעזשקע פֿון די מאַשינביקסן
פֿון די ליטווישע פּאַרטיזאַנער. אָקטאָבער 4: קאָוונע, נײַנטער פֿאָרט —
315 יׅידישע מענער, 712 יׅידישע פֿרויען,

818 יׅידישע קינדער (אַ שטראָף־אַקציע ווײַל
אַ דײַטשישער פּאָליציסט איז דערשאָסן געוואָרן אין געטאָ). אָקטאָבער 29:
קאָוונע, נײַנטער פֿאָרט — 2,007 יׅידישע מענער, 2,920 יׅידישע פֿרויען,
4,273 יׅידישע קינדער (אַרויסגענומען פֿון געטאָ מחמת אַן עודף איבעריקע יׅידן),
אויסגראָבן און פֿאַרברענען. ווער עס איז
באַגראָבן געוואָרן האָט געמוזט אויסגעגראָבן ווערן. דער פֿײַער־מײַסטער,
דער עקספּערט פֿון פֿאַרברענען האָט אָנגעפֿירט מיט די פֿײַערלמײַ,
דרײַ הונדערט קערפֿערס אַרויסגעגראָבן און פֿאַרברענט

יעדן טאָג ביז דער שטויב פֿון די מתים איז פֿאַרשווונדן
אין דער ערד אָדער זיך צעפֿלויגן אין דער לופֿט אין די הייכן.

73

7

In the cemetery at Keidan the stones
are covered with moss and earth. You pick
leaves, a handful of stems and broad leaves
wide across as your two hands
and you scrub the surface
of stone clean. You take leaves
from the moist earth and kneel
down and make an opening in the moss

and earth until the carved letters speak again.
Like a bright face, the names are whole, we say
them aloud.   Sometimes at night,
if I take the magnifying glass and enter the forest
of Ponar or climb above the River Obelis,
walk in the newly formed woods, a few grave stones left
for the resting dead, if I put my face close
to the photograph, it seems I can enter

there with my body. That I am there.
Now I look closely at their faces, those
who guard the entrance to the town of Datnuva
where once my family grew flax and made linen,
they guard their cache of pears, apples, cucumbers,
cabbage, cherries. I want to ask...
oh at night how I long to ask them
to tell me about my family if I promise

אויפֿן בית־עולם אין קיידאַן זענען די מצבֿות
באַדעקט מיט מאָך און ערד. דו קלײַבסט צונויף
בלעטער, אַ הויפֿן שטענגלעך און ברייטע בלעטער
אַרום זיך װי װײַט דײַנע הענט גרייכן
און דו שמײַערסט אָפּ די אײַבערפֿלאַך
פֿון דער מצבֿה אויף זויבעררײן. דו נעמסט בלעטער
פֿון דעם פֿײַכטן באָדן און שטעלסט זיך אויף די קני
און מאַכסט אויף אַן עפֿענונג אין דעם מאָך

און דער ערד ביז אויסגעציזילירטע אותיות באַװײַזן זיך װידער.
װי אַ ליכטיק פּנים, װערן די נעמען גאַנץ, מיר לייענען
זיי אויף אַ קול, צו מאָל אין דער נאַכט,
אויב איך נעם דאָס פֿאַרגרעסער־גלאָז און גיי אַרײַן אין װאַלד
פֿון פּאַנאַר אָדער אַרויף צום אַבעלע טײַכל,
גיי דורך די נײַ געפֿלאַנצטע ביימער, װוּ עטלעכע מצבֿות זענען געבליבן
פֿאַר דער מנוחה פֿון די מתים,
זעט עס אויס װי כ'װאָלט קענען אַרײַן

אהין מיט מײַן גוף. און איך בין טאַקע דאָרטן,
איצט קוק איך אָן די פּנימער פֿון דער נאָענט, די
װאָס באַװאַכן דעם אַרײַנגאַנג צום שטעטל דאָטנעװוע
װוּ אַ מאָל האָט מײַן משפּחה דאָרטן געלאָזט װאַקסן פֿלאַקס און געמאַכט לײַװנט.
זיי האָבן די שמירה איבערן באַהעלטער פֿון באַרנעס, עפּל, אוגערקעס,
קרויט, קאַרשן. איך װיל פֿרעגן . . .
אָ, װי עס ציט מײַן הארץ אין דער נאַכט זיי צו בעטן
מיר צו דערצײַלן פֿון מײַן משפּחה אויב כ'װעל צוזאָגן

Josvainiai: Wolpe gravestone. Photo credit: Myra Sklarew

not to judge them. At night I clear
a space around this as if I were
going on a long journey and must leave
things in good order,
in readiness for someone else.
I want the center to open. Nothing
to interfere. The way at night I open
the package and take out the pictures

and with a magnifying glass
enter the green world inside,
as though my body has physically
moved into their spaces, as though
I am once again in Lithuania.
In this courtyard where once the living
dreamed as you dream: touch
this leaf, that strong trunk.

Touch the petals of the poppy
as they did. Perhaps someone has left you
a message, a strip of bark torn away
by a finger, now high over you
in that birch. Go on, go down.
Go further on. A child said: I want to be
a dog. A child said: I hid here.
A child said: I could not hide here.

ניט צו פֿסקענען וועגן זיי. אין דער נאַכט קלאָר איך אויס
אָן אָרט אַרום דעם אַלעם אַזוי ווי כ'וואָלט זיך קלײַבן
אַרויסגיין אויף אַ ווײַטער נסיעה און מוז איבערלאָזן
זאַכן דאָ אין בעסטער אָרדענונג,
צוגעגרייט פֿאַר עמעצן אַנדערש.
איך וויל דער צענטער זאָל זיך עפֿענען. קיין זאַך
זאָל ניט שטערן, דער אופֿן ווי אין דער נאַכט עפֿן איך
דאָס פֿעקל און נעם אַרויס די בילדער

און מיט אַ פֿאַרגרעסער־גלאָז
גיי איך אַרײַן אין דער גרינער וועלט אינעווייניק,
גלײַך ווי מײַן קערפער וואָלט פֿיזיש
אַרײַנגעדרונגען אין זייערע סֿערע, גלײַך ווי
איך וואָלט ווידער אַ מאָל געוואָרן אין ליטע.
אין דעם הויף ווו אַ מאָל האָבן די לעבעדיקע
געחלומט אָט אַזוי ווי דו חלומסט: באַריר
דעם בלאַט, דעם פֿעסטן שטאַם.

באַריר די קרוינבלעטלעך פֿון דעם מאָן
ווי זיי פֿלעגן עס טאָן. אפֿשר האָט עמעץ פֿאַר דיר איבערגעלאָזן
אַ סימן: אַ פֿאַסיקל קאָרע אַוועקגעריסן
פֿון אַ פֿינגער, איז איצט הויך איבער דיר
אין דער בעריאָזע. גיי זיך דעם וועג. גיי אַראָפ,
זע ממשיך דײַן גאַנג, אַ קינד האָט געזאָגט: איך וויל ווערן
אַ הינטל. אַ קינד האָט געזאָגט: איך וועל זיך דאָ באַהאַלטן,
אַ קינד האָט געזאָגט: דאָ קען איך זיך ניט באַהאַלטן.

A woman in Girkalnis, for
offering food and water to the Jews,
was locked up with them
in the cloister of her church
without water or food until some
went mad. Until they were taken
to a pit and massacred, the little ones
hung by their feet and broken

against trees. At Ponar
there are flowers that grow
over the mass graves, ghost
flowers, mutants with nature's colors
wrung out of them, their white
stamens tipped in blood.
The harvest holiday was kept
in October. It was celebrated

in the forest and all in the village took
part, bringing the dark bread, beer. Animals
were sacrificed to the gods. The souls
of the dead were invited home
and provided spare chairs and towels.
Tables were filled with food and drink
for the returning souls.
After the souls were cared for, the villagers

א פֿרוי אין גירקלאָן, פֿאַר

צוברענגען שפּײַז און וואַסער צו די ייִדן,

איז פֿאַרשפּאַרט געוואָרן מיט זיי צוזאַמען

אין דעם מאָנאַסטיר פֿון קלויסטער

אָן וואַסער און אָן עסנוואַרג ביז עטלעכע

זענען אַראָפּ פֿון זינען. צום סוף האָט מען זיי גענומען

צו אַ גרוב און דאָרטן געפּײַניקט. דאָס קלײַנוואַרג

האָט מען אויפֿגעהאַנגען פֿאַר די פֿיס און זיי צעשמעטערט

אָן די ביימער. אין פֿאָנאַר

דאָרט זענען פֿאַראַן בלומען וואָס וואַקסן

אויף די מאַסן־קבֿרים, שדים־

בלומען אַנדערשדיק פֿאַרביטן מיט דער נאַטורס קאָלירן

וואָס דראַפּען זיך אַרויס פֿון זייערע וועמסע

שטויבפֿאָעדעם אָנגעפֿינטלט מיט בלוט.

דער גערעטעניש־פֿעסטיוואַל איז אָפֿגעהאַלטן געוואָרן

אין אָקטאָבער. עס איז געפֿײַערט געוואָרן

אין דעם וואַל און דער גאַנצער דאַרף האָט גענומען

אָנטייל. מע האָט מיטגעבראַכט שוואַרצן ברויט, ביר. בהמות

זענען געשאָכטן געוואָרן אַ קרבן צו די געטער. די נשמות

פֿון די טויטע זענען פֿאַרבעטן געוואָרן אַהיים

און פֿאַרזאָרגט געוואָרן מיט אַ צוגאָב פֿון שטולן און האַנטטיכער.

די טישן זענען פֿול אָנגעשטעלט געוואָרן מיט מאכלים און שנאַפּס

פֿאַר די צוריקקומענדיקע נשמות.

נאָך דעם ווי די נשמות זענען געוואָרן פֿאַרזאָרגט, האָבן די פּויערים

bathed themselves in the river.
They called the liquidation
of the Jews *Erntefest*—harvest festival.
Later, when it was done,
and the land which rested in the confluence
of two great rivers was covered
with water, the inhabitants
grew fearful and went to the cemetery

and took off the Jews' clothing.
They threw the belongings
of the dead Jews over the fence
into the cemetery in order to make
the flood waters recede. In Slobodka,
the headless body of the chief rabbi was found
still seated near an open volume of the Talmud
he had been studying. In those days

it was said that if you removed
the head of a people, then it was not difficult
to destroy the body.

זיך אויסגעבבאָדן אין טײַך,
זיי האָבן אָנגערופֿן דאָס אומברענגען
פֿון די ייִדן ערנטעפֿעסט — גערעטעניש יום־טובֿ.
שפּעטער, ווען ס'איז אַלץ געווען פֿאַרענדיקט,
און דאָס לאַנד וואָס האָט גערוט אין צוזאַמענשטראַם
פֿון צוויי גרויסע טײַכן איז פֿאַרטרונקען געוואָרן
פֿון וואַסער, האָבן די אײַנוווינערס
זיך שטאַרק דערשראָקן און זענען אַוועק צום בית־עולם

און האָבן די ייִדן אויסגעטאָן די בגדים
זיי האָבן דאָס האָב־און־גוטס
פֿון די טויטע ייִדן אַריבערגעוואָרפֿן איבערן גדר
אינעם בית־הקבֿרות כּדי צו מאַכן
אַז דאָס געוויסער זאָל אָפּפֿאַלן. אין סלאַבאַדקע
האָט מען געפֿונען דעם אָנקעפּיקן גוף פֿון עלטערן רבֿ
נאָך זיצנדיק איבער אַ מסכתּא פֿון דער גמרא
וואָס ער האָט געהאַלטן אין לערנען. אין יענע צײַטן

האָבן זיי געגלייבט אַז אויב מע נעמט אַראָפּ
דעם קאָפּ פֿון אַ מענטשן, איז שוין ניט שווער
צו פֿאַרניכטן דעם גוף.

What I remember is not how they were
rounded up like animals, caught
like fish in a net, beaten and shouted at, dragged
over the fallen bodies of their kind, not how
they stood against a wall or at the edge
of a ravine or a pit or a trench they themselves
were forced to dig, knowing
it was for their own graves, not how they were

bludgeoned or blasted out of this life,
nor what they thought or felt as they breathed
in the air of their last moments, but
what happened afterward. The single human
acts that came afterwards. We know about the killings,
we have seen the pictures, read the descriptions, heard
the testimonies. We know nothing about the killings.
How could we? But what happened afterward.

How the women who were not burned
alive in the school house or the church or their villages
sent the smallest children home and walked up
to the edge of the ravine to see
for themselves. How they stepped carefully
among the bodies until they found their own: brothers, sons,
fathers. How they tenderly held their hands,
their heads, still warm. How they did not know

וואָס איך געדענק איז ניט ווי זיי זענען
אַרומגערינגלט געוואָרן ווי חיות, געכאַפּט געוואָרן
ווי פֿיש אין אַ נעץ, צעשלאָגן און אָנגעגוואַלדעוועט, געשלעפּט געוואָרן
איבער די איינער אויפֿן אַנדערן אָנגעפֿאַלענע קערפּערס פֿון די זייעריקע. ניט ווי
זיי שטייען קעגנאיבער אַ וואַנט אָדער בײַם ברעג
פֿון אַ ראָוו צי אַ גרוב צי אַ טראַנשעע וואָס זיי אַליין
האָבן געצוווּנגענערהייט אויסגעגראָבן, וויסנדיק
אַז דאָס זענען זייערע אייגענע קבֿרים. ניט ווי זיי זענען געוואָרן

אַרויסגעקלאַפּט און אַרויסגעריסן פֿון דער לעבעדיקער וועלט,
ניט וואָס זיי האָבן געטראַכט אָדער געפֿילט בעת זיי האָבן אַמאַנגעטאַעמט
די לופֿט אין זייערע לעצטע רגעס, אָבער
וואָס נאָך דעם האָט פֿאַסירט די איינציקע מענטשלעכע
מעשים וואָס זענען געקומען נאָך דעם. מיר ווייסן וועגן די הריגות,
מיר האָבן געזען די בילדער, געלייענט די באַשרײַבוגגען, געהערט
דאָס עדותשאַפֿט. ערשט מיר ווייסן מיר באַנעמען גאָרנישט ניט פֿון דעם אומקום,
ווי אַזוי עס פֿאַרשטיין? אָבער דאָס וואָס האָט פֿאַסירט נאָך דעם.

ווי די פֿרויען וואָס זענען ניט פֿאַרברענט געוואָרן
לעבעדיקערהייט אין שול־בנין אָדער אין קלויסטער אָדער אין זייערע ישובֿים
האָבן געשיקט די קלענערע קינדער אַהיים און אַליין צוגעקומען
צום ראַנד פֿון דער גרוב אָנצוקוקן
מיט די אייגענע אויגן. ווי אָפּגעהיט זיי האָבן געטראָטן
צווישן די קערפּערס ביז זיי האָבן געפֿונען זייערע אייגענע: ברידער, זין,
מיט וואָס פֿאַראַ צאַרטקייט זיי האָבן געגלעט זייערע הענט,
זייערע קעפּ, וואָס זענען נאָך געווען וואַרעם. ווי זיי האָבן ניט געוווּסט

what to do. How they removed the wedding rings
from the fingers before they grew stiff and wore,
from that day on, two rings on their wedding finger.
How that night they came with candles
and kept a vigil so their dear ones would not
be alone all night. How in the morning they came with water
and cloths and washed their dead and prepared them
for burial. How they carried each of them on a palette

to the graveyard, 1300 of them. How the other villagers
came to help them. And they set them in the center
of the cemetery and with the stones of the stony fields
they built a wall around them, to keep them from wild
animals, to give them the burial every dead one deserves.
But for mine, the tender acts afterward were not
possible, not the hands on their faces, nor the white
cloths to wash them, nor a few drops of water,

nor their faces turned upward to the opening
sky, but thrown down, eyes wide against the blood earth,
in whatever state they happened to fall, whatever moment
of surprise or pain. Nor were there any to find them, to carry
them, to console my dead. Afterward, to cover these actions,
those barely alive were forced to dig the bodies up
out of the pits, to prepare a place for burning, a stack of logs, a row
of bodies, logs, bodies, orderly but for the power of the odor

of death, but for the decay of death, the fires taking them,
taking the living, not even washing
the dead, not even burying our dead, not even, not

וואָס צו טאָן, ווי זיי האָבן אַרפגענומען די קידושין־רינגען
פֿון די פֿינגערס אײדער זיי װערן פֿאַרשטאַפֿט און צעפֿאַלן.
פֿון אָט דעם טאָג, זענען געװען צװײ קידושין־רינגעלעך אױפֿן פֿינגער.
װי אין דער זעלביקער נאַכט זענען זיי געקומען מיט ליכט
און געװאָאַכט אַז זײערע ליבסטע זאָלן ניט
זײַן אַלײן אַ גאַנצע נאַכט. װי אין פֿרימאָרגן זענען זיי געקומען מיט װאַסער
און לײװנט און געװאָשן זײערע מתים און זיי צוגעגרײט
צו קבורה. װי זיי האָבן יעדן באַזונדער געטראָגן אױף אַ שטרױמאַטראַץ

צום בית־עולם, 1300 זענען זיי געװען. װי אַנדערע פֿױערים
זענען געקומען זיי העלפֿן. און זיי האָבן זיי אַװעקגעלײגט אין מיטן
פֿון בית־עלמין און מיט די שטײנער פֿון די שטײנערדיקע פֿעלדער
האָבן זיי אױיסגעבױיט אַ װאַנט אַרום זיי, צו באַשיצן פֿון װילדע
חיות, זיי געבראַכט צו קבורה װי עס קומט יעדן מת.
אָבער פֿאַר די מײַניקע, זענען די מעשׂי־חסד נאָך דעם ניט געװען
מעגלעך, ניט זיי צומאַכן די אױגן, ניט די װאַסע
תכריכים און ניט זיי מטהר זײַן, ניט אַפֿילו עטלעכע װאַסער־טראָפֿנס,

ניט מיט זײערע פֿינגער צוגעקערט צום אױבן צום אָפֿענעם
הימל, נאָר אַראָפּגעשלײַדערט אַראָפּ צו, מיט אױיפֿגעריסענע אױיגן צו דער בלוטיקער ע
װי ס'איז זיי באַשערט געװען צו פֿאַלן, װי עס זאָל ניט זײַן די רגע
פֿון פֿלוצעמדיקייט און יסורים. ניט געװען דאָרט װער עס זאָל זיי זוכן, טראָגן
זיי, געבן מײַנע מתים אַ טרײיסטער. נאָך דעם, צו מאַסקירן זײַערע מעשׂים,
זענען די נאָך קױם לעבעדיקע געצױוונגען געװאָרן אױיסצוגראַבן די קעפֿערס פֿון די
גריבער, פֿון די ראָוס, צוגרײיטן אַן אָרט זיי צו פֿאַרברײענען, אַ שטױיס מיט קלעצער,
אַ רײ פֿון גופֿים, קלעצער, גופֿים, מיט אַ סדר נאָר די שטאַרקייט פֿון דעם

אַװיר פֿון טױיט, די צעפֿױילונג פֿון מתים, די פֿײַערן פֿאַרכאַפֿן זײ,
פֿאַרכאַפֿן די לעבעדיקע, אַפֿילו ניט מטהר געװען
די מתים. אַפֿילו ניט געבראַכט צו קבורת־ישראל אונזערע טױיטע, אַפֿילו ניט, ניט

When Joseph caught sight of his
brothers tending their father's flock
in Dothan, he approached eagerly. *Behold,*
they said, seeing their young brother
in the distance: *Here comes our little dreamer.*
They conspired to slay the boy, to throw
him into a pit. Later they will say
to their father: *An animal has devoured*

your son Joseph. A father is pointing
to the sky. He is stroking the boy's head.
An old woman is singing to the baby
in her arms. The SS guard at the pit shouts
something to his comrade. We cannot hear
what he says. The family climbs down into the pit,
lines up against the dead. For those who cannot
walk, others already naked carry the fragile

bodies of the still living into the pit. Here in America
a child asks—Why is there an earthquake?
Is it because God wants to punish
the earth?—all the while moving her head
first to one side, then to the other like the periscope
of a submarine, feeling the air with her head.
As she speaks another temblor
passes through the earth.

In Keidan, the earth of the trench where the murdered were buried
seems to pull away from the surrounding earth as if the sacred burial
place could not bear to touch the adjacent soil.

ווען יוסף האָט געכאַפּט אַ קוק אויף זײַנע
ברידער וואָס פּאַשען זייער פֿאַטערס טשערעדעס
אין דותן, האָט ער זיך דערנענטערט אומוויליק, זע,
האָבן זיי געזאָגט, דערקענענדיק זייער יונגן ברודער
פֿון דער ווײַטן: אָט קומט אונדזער קליינער בעל־חלומות.
זיי האָבן זיך פֿאַרשוואָרן אַוועקצוהרגענען דאָס יינגל, אַרײַנצוּוואַרפֿן
אים אין אַ גרוב. שפּעטער וועלן זיי דערציילן
זייער פֿאַטער: אַ ווילדע חיה האָט פֿאַרצוקט

דײַן זון יוסף. אַ טאַטע טײַטלט
צום הימל. ער גלעט דעם יינגלס קאָפּ.
אַן אַלטע פֿרוי זינגט צום עופֿעלע
אין אירע אָרעמס. דער עס־עס. וואַכפאַסטן בײַ דער גרוב שרײַט
עפּעס צו זײַן קאַמעראַד. מיר קענען ניט אויפֿכאַפֿן
וואָס ער זאָגט. די משפחה קריכט אַרונטער אין גרוב,
שטעלט זיך אין רײ הינטער די מתים. פֿאַר די וואָס קענען ניט
גיין. די אַנדערע וואָס זענען שוין נאַקעט טראָגן די קרוכלע

קערפּערס פֿון די נאָך לעבעדיקע אין גרוב אַראָפּ. דאָ אין אַמעריקע
פֿרעגט אַ קינד — פֿאַרוואָס איז דאָרטן אַן ערדציטערניש?
איז עס מחמת גאָט וויל באַשטראָפֿן
די ערד? — בעת־מעשׂה שאָקלענדיק איר קאָפּ
צו ערשט צו איין זײַט, נאָך דעם צו דער צווייטער ווי דער פֿעריסקאָפּ
פֿון אַ סובמאַרין, אָפּפֿילנדיק די לופֿט מיט איר קאָפּ.
ווי זי האַלט אין ריידן איז נאָך אַ טרייסלעניש
גייט דורך דורך דער ערד.

אין קיידאַן, די ערד פֿון טראַנשעע ווו די אויסגעמאָרדטע זענען
באַגראָבן זעט אויס ווי ווי זי וואָלט זיך אָפּצִיען פֿון דער ערד ארום ווי דער
הייליקער קבורה־פּלאַץ וואָלט ניט פֿאַרטראָגן דעם באַריר פֿון דערבײַיקן באָדן.

Ponar Excavation. Photo credit: Myra Sklarew

10

What is the nature of the pit which has been made?
With what instruments was it dug? Or with whose bare
hands? And what was encountered in the earth
when the digging commenced? Who prepared
the pit? And did they stand back to back,
or in rows? Did they work in stages or in shifts?
And who commanded the digging. Was there one pit
or many? Did the people walk of their own accord

from the barricaded trains to the pit
or were they beaten and whipped as they were driven
off the trains? Were they dead or alive
when they entered the pit? Were the pits dug
by the Russians for the storage of oil?
Or by the Lithuanians for the bodies of Jews?
Or by the Jews? When the Jews were sent
from Kovno to Slobodka—30,000 to fit

into the space for 7,000— the Germans
required 50 the first day and 100 the next
to build the barbed wire fence—first
the ghetto, then a concentration camp
which would be their route to death.
A man remembers a Russian song: "Bricklayer,
bricklayer, for whom do you lay these bricks?
We have no time to tell you. We are busy

וואָס איז אין דער נאַטור פֿון דער גרוב וואָס איז דאָ געמאַכט געוואָרן?
מיט וועלכע מכשירים איז זי אויסגעגראָבן געוואָרן? אָדער מיט וועמעס נאָקעטע
הענט? און אין וואָס האָט מען זיך אָנגעשטויסן אין דער ערד
ווען דאָס גראָבן האָט זיך פֿאַרענדיקט? ווער האָט צוגעגרייט
די גרוב? און זענען זיי געשטאַנען רוקן צו רוקן,
אָדער אין רייען? האָבן זיי געאַרבעט אין פֿאַזעס אָדער אין שיכטן?
און ווער האָט באַפֿעלט איבער דאָס גראָבן, איז דאָרטן געווען איין גרוב
אָדער אַ סך? זענען די מענטשן געגאַנגען מיטן אייגענעם ווילן

פֿון די פֿאַרהאַקטע וואַגאָנען צו דער גרוב
אָדער זענען זיי צעמומיתע און צעשמיסן געוואָרן בעתן טרײַבן
פֿון די באַנען? זענען זיי געווען טויט צי לעבעדיק
ווען זיי זענען אַרײַן אין גרוב? זענען די גריבער געגראָבן געוואָרן
פֿון די רוסן אויף צו לאָגערן פֿעטראָל?
אָדער פֿון די ליטווינער פֿאַר די קערפֿערס פֿון ייִדן?
אָדער פֿון די ייִדן? ווען זיי זענען אַרויסגעטריבן געוואָרן
פֿון קאָוונע צו סלאַבאָדקע — 30,000 אַרײַנצופֿאַסן

אויף אַ שטח פֿאַר 7,000 — די דײַטשן
האָבן פֿאַרלאַנגט 50 דעם ערשטן טאָג און 100 דעם אַנדערן
אויפֿצושטעלן דעם צוים פֿון שטעכלדראָט — צו ערשט
די געטאָ, נאָך דעם אַ קאָנצענטראַציע־לאַגער
וואָס האָט געזאָלט זײַן דער גאַנג צום טויט.
אַ ייִד געדענקט אַ רוסיש לידל: „מויערער,
מולער, פֿאַר וועמען לייגסטו די ציגל?
מיר האָבן קיין צײַט ניט צו שמועסן, מיר זענען פֿאַרנומען

93

Helen Verblunsky in the Kovno Ghetto. Helen's mother, Tova, a member of a forced labor brigade, smuggled milk into the ghetto, which she obtained from Lithuanians in exchange for articles of clothing. Both survived the war. Photo credit: George Kadish, courtesy of the USHMM Photo Archives.

Yankel (Yaakov) Meryash works the lathe in the ORT metal works shop in the Ghetto. Behind him at the left is Max Wolpe. Both boys survived and live in Israel. Photo credit: Avraham Tory, courtesy of the USHMM Photo Archives.

building a prison for ourselves."
What are the true dimensions of a pit?
How deep is a pit which must hold
50,000 people? Shall they be murdered facing up
or facing down? How shall their clothes
be sorted afterward? Or shall they be required
to place their clothing in the correct
piles beforehand: shoes in one pile,

underclothes in another, outer
clothing in a third. At Ponar some went down alive
into the pit, a fine covering of earth
closed about them. And they perished.
And some went down alive and no covering
of earth came to them. And some
who were devoured in the earth were brought up
to the light once more to be set

ablaze in the light of burning. Of these
there was found a mother holding the hand
of her child. *My days are past,*
my purposes broken off…if I look for the nether-world
as my house, if I have spread my couch
in the darkness, if I have said to corruption: Thou
art my father, to the worm: Thou art my mother,
and my sister, Where then is my hope.

He hath fenced up my way that I cannot pass.
He hath broken me down on every side and
I am gone and my hope hath He plucked up like a tree.

מיר בויען אַ טורמע פֿאַר זיך אַליין".
וואָס זענען די אמתע אויסמעסטונגען פֿון אַ גרוב?
ווי טיף איז אַ גרוב וואָס זאָל אַרײַננעמען
50,000 מענטשן? דאַרפֿן זיי אויסגעהרגעט ווערן מיטן פּנים אַרויף
אָדער מיטן פּנים אַראָפּ? ווי דאַרפֿן זייערע ע בגדים
נאָך דעם סאָרטירט ווערן? אָדער דאַרף מען זיי באַפֿעלן
אויסצוסדרן זייערע קליידער אין ריכטיקע
הויפֿנס אַפֿריִער נאָך: שיך אין איין הויפֿן,

אונטערוועש אין אַן אנדערן, אייבערשטע
בגדים אין אַ דריטן. אין פֿאָנאַר זענען עטלעכע אַראָפּ לעבעדיק
אין דער גרוב, אַ דינער שיכט ערד
האָט זיי פֿאַרדעקט. און זיי זענען אומגעקומען.
און אַ ביסל זענען אַראָפּ לעבעדיקע און קיין צודעק
פֿון ערד איז אויבער זיי ניט אַראָפּגעפֿאַלן. און אַ טייל
פֿאַרשלונגענע אין דער ערד זענען אַרויפֿגעבראַכט געוואָרן
צו דער ליכטיקער שײַן נאָך אַ מאָל צו ווערן אַרויפֿגעלייגט

אויף די צעפֿאַלקערטע פּלאַמען פֿון שמײַטער. צווישן זיי
איז געווען אַ מאַמע וואָס האַלט די האַנט
פֿון איר קינד. מײַנע טעג זענען פֿאַרגאַנגען,
מײַנע געדאַנקען זענען צעריסן . . . אַז איך ריכט זיך אויף דער אונטערערד
ווי מײַן היים, אין פֿינצטערניש בעט איך אויס
מײַן געלעגער, צום קבֿר רוף איך: דו
ביסט מײַן פֿאָטער, צום וואָרעם: דו ביסט מײַן מוטער
און מײַן שוועסטער, ווי איז דען מײַן האָפֿענונג.

מײַן וועג האָט ער פֿאַרצאַמט אַז איך קען ניט דורכגיין.
ער האָט מיך צעבראָכן פֿון אַלע זײַטן און
איך פֿאַרגיי און ווי ווי אַ בוים האָט ער אויסגעריסן מײַן האָפֿענונג.

97

About the Author

Myra Sklarew, former president of the artists' community Yaddo, is professor of literature and co-director of the MFA Program in Creative Writing at American University. She is the author of eight books of poetry and a collection of short fiction. *From the Backyard of the Diaspora* received the Jewish Book Council Award in Poetry in 1977. *Eating the White Earth* was translated into Hebrew in 1994. Forthcoming work includes a non-fiction study of the Holocaust and the construction of memory and a collection of essays, *From Mole Hills to Messiah*. Ms. Sklarew's poetry has been recorded for the Library of Congress' Archive of Poetry and Literature.

About the Yiddish Translator

David Wolpe is an internationally acclaimed writer, poet, cultural activist, literary critic and scholar who was born in 1908 in Keidan, Lithuania. He studied at the Tarbut-Gimnazie before immigrating to Israel in 1930. In 1937, he returned to Lithuania and during the war lived in the Slobodka Ghetto before being sent to the Dachau concentration camp. After the war, he lived in the Munchen Displaced Persons Camp before immigrating to South Africa in 1951.

Mr. Wolpe has published articles for the Yiddish magazines *Muchener Undzer Veg, Dos Vort, Yiddishe Tsaytung, Bafrayung, Undzer Velt, Afrikaner Yiddishe Tsaytung, Goldene Keyt,* and *Yiddish Kultur.* From 1955 through 1970 he was the editor of the magazine *Dorem Afrike.* He is the author of *A Volkn Un a Veg, Songs and Poems, A Vort in Zayn Tsayt, Iber Zayn Libervelt* a book he co-authored with Abraham Sutzkever, and two additional volumes of poetry that he published in 1998 and 1999. He recently published a two volume autobiography, *I and My World.*

David Wolpe is the winner of the Itzik Manger Prize in 1983 and the Chaim Zhitlovsky Prize in 1996. He currently lives in Johannesburg with his family.